Essay Writing A To Z
STEP 2_ Essay Types

Steve Brown

Steve Brown is a qualified TEFL (Teaching English as a Foreign Language) instructor and has taught IELTS, TOEFL, TOEIC and general English in Asia, Europe and South America. He has authored numerous English language textbooks, including the "Writing Master" series for Nexus Publishing. Before teaching, Steve worked as a stockbroker and regulatory consultant in London (UK). He is an alumnus of the Chartered Institute for Securities Professionals.

Hee Cho

Hee Cho has post-graduate degrees in English Linguistics from both Sogang University (Korea) and Birmingham University (UK), and also in International Public Relations from the University of Cardiff (UK). She currently works as a professor of English Test tuition on behalf of Kangnam University's Pathway program in collaboration with the University of Canberra (Australia), and as a tutor at Imperial College London in the UK. Previously Hee has taught at Sogang, Dongyang Mirae, and Duksung Women's universities in Korea, as well as teaching TOEFL at CYJ(정이조) Academy in Seoul. She has a number of published works, including "I love NEAT speaking" for EBS Publishing.

Essay Writing A To Z
STEP 2_ Essay Types

First published in August 2012 by
Saramin Publishing Co., Inc.
378-16, Seogyo-dong, Mapo-gu,
Seoul, Korea 121-894
Tel: 82-2-338-3555
Fax: 82-2-338-3545

Copyright © 2012 Steve Brown & Hee Cho

All rights reserved. This publication may not be reproduced, stored, or distributed in any form or by any means, electronic or mechanical, including photocopying, recording or otherwise, without the prior written permission of the publisher.

Authors Steve Brown, Hee Cho

Publisher Hyosang Park
Editors Jinjoo Cho, Heejin Mo, Jongman Lee, Woonhee Park
Designers Jungsu Son, Youngseon Yoon
Marketing Jongseon Lee, Taeho Lee, Jeonhee Lee

Design by Jungyoon Cho

ISBN 978-89-6049-325-4 13740
978-89-6049-323-0 (set)
Components Student's Book / Answers

Price 13,800 won
www.saramin.com
*Unit Summary in Korean and Teacher's PowerPoint presentation are available.

Write the Greatest Essays

Essay Writing A to Z

STEP 2 **Essay Types**
Steve Brown · Hee Cho

saramin

Introduction

What Is in This Book?

Whether you are writing an essay for a university assignment, for TOEFL or for IELTS, you are often answering the same type of question. You might need to give your opinion, agree or disagree with something, or compare some advantages and disadvantages. This book shows you the key skills you need to write each type of essay, how to structure your answers, and how to write clearly and efficiently.

Why Is This Book Different from Other 'Essay Writing' Books?

1 Each unit examines real essays and passages written by Korean students of English.

2 Each unit contains multiple exercises in addition to a step-by-step guide regarding the topic.

3 The book is equally useful as a textbook for teachers or as a self-study workbook.

Introduction

Who Is This Book for?

This book is aimed at intermediate level students of English who:

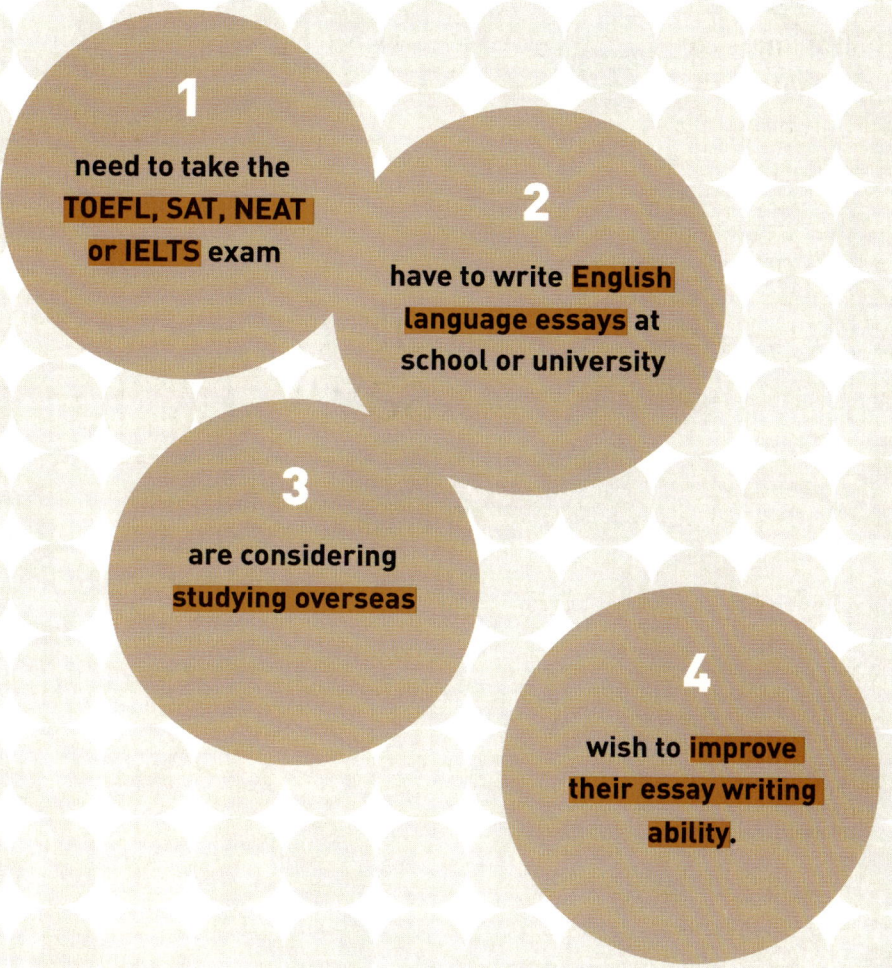

1. need to take the TOEFL, SAT, NEAT or IELTS exam
2. have to write English language essays at school or university
3. are considering studying overseas
4. wish to improve their essay writing ability.

The book assumes you can read, understand and write English at an intermediate level, and it assumes you already know terms such as 'brainstorming' and 'outlining.'

Introduction

How Is the Book Structured?

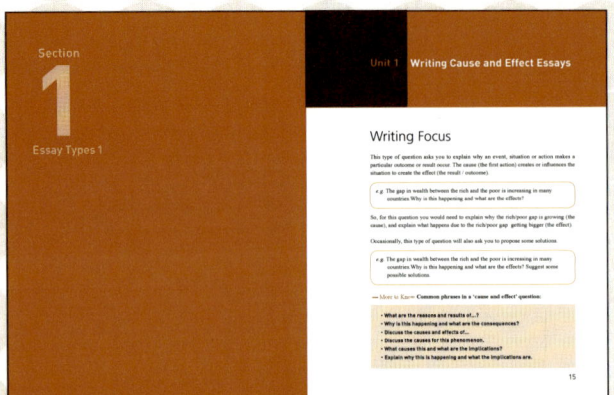

Section 1 Essay Types 1 analyzes 3 main types of essay: cause and effect, advantages/disadvantages, compare and contrast, and looks at the key skills required for each type.

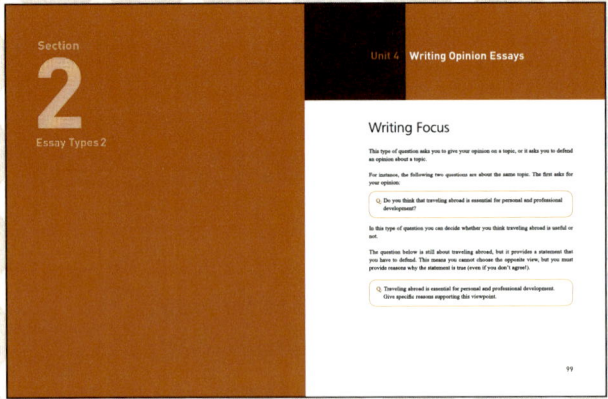

Section 2 Essay Types 2 analyzes the other main types of essay: opinion, preference, agree/disagree, and looks at the key skills required for each type.

Introduction

How is Each Unit Structured?

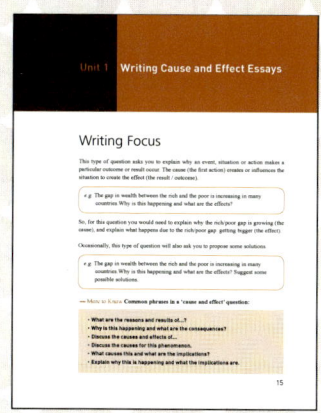

Writing Focus
provides an easy-to-understand explanation of the topic.

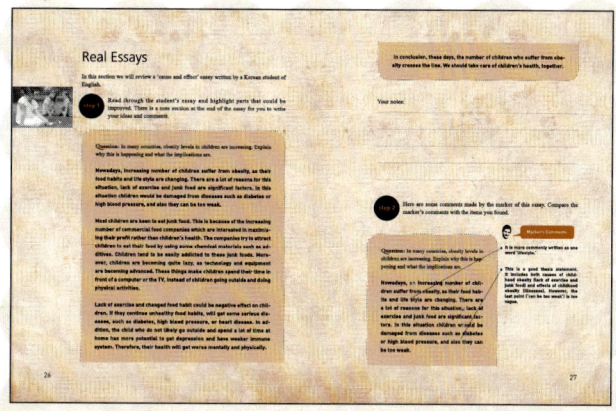

Real Essays
examines the writing of a Korean student of English.

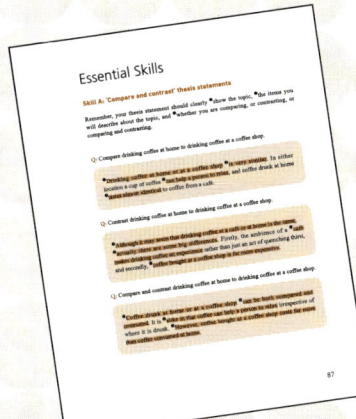

Essential Skills
looks at the essential skills needed for the topic.

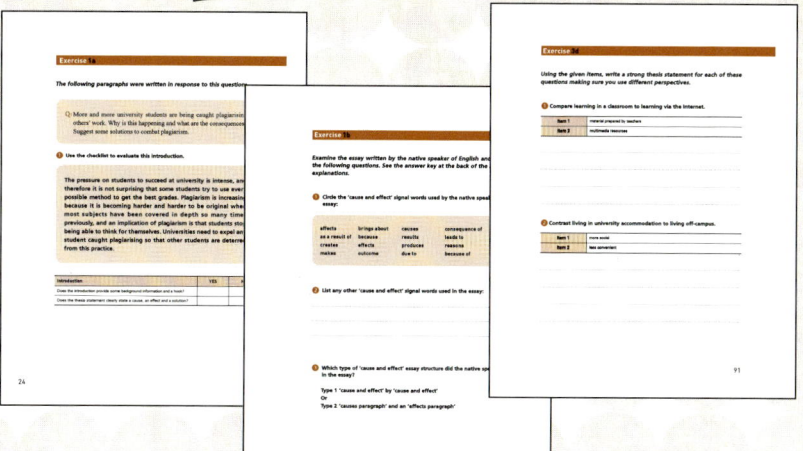

Multiple Exercises
helps you understand the topic and gives you a chance to practice the topic.

At the back of the book there is an Answer Guide that provides not only the answers to the exercises, but also comprehensive explanations.

Introduction

Thank you!

This book contains sentences, passages and essays written by Korean learners of English. These students generously agreed to allow us to use their writing so that others may improve their English ability.

We would like to say a big 'thank you' to:

Seung Min	Hyo Jae	Sun Ho	Seu Reo Woon
Seung Eun	Jeong Jun	Da Eun	Ji Su
Hae Rim	Nan Hee	Jeong Whan	Min Hyeok
Da Hyeong	Yoo Kyung		

Steve Brown & Hee Cho

Contents STEP 2

Section 1 Essay Types 1 _13

Unit	Features
1 Writing Cause and Effect Essays _15	▶ Explanation and common question phrases ▶ How to answer this type of question ▶ Structuring the essay ▶ Analysis of writing by Korean students of English ▶ Essential skills: difference between a cause and an effect, linking causes and effects ▶ Multiple exercises
2 Writing Advantages/ Disadvantages Essays _43	▶ Explanation and common question phrases ▶ How to answer this type of question ▶ Structuring the essay ▶ Analysis of writing by Korean students of English ▶ Essential skills: essay statements, not giving preferences or opinions ▶ Multiple exercises
3 Writing Compare and Contrast Essays _67	▶ Explanation and common question phrases ▶ How to answer this type of question ▶ Structuring the essay ▶ Analysis of writing by Korean students of English ▶ Essential skills: compare/contrast thesis statements, comparing and contrasting from different perspectives ▶ Multiple exercises

Contents STEP 2

Section 2 Essay Types 2 _97

Unit	Features
4 Writing Opinion Essays _99	▶ Explanation and common question phrases ▶ How to answer this type of question ▶ Structuring the essay ▶ Analysis of writing by Korean students of English ▶ Essential skills: writing clear and precise opinions, validating your opinions ▶ Multiple exercises
5 Writing Preference Essays _125	▶ Explanation and common question phrases ▶ How to answer this type of question ▶ Structuring the essay ▶ Analysis of writing by Korean students of English ▶ Essential skills: acknowledging other statements or opinions, expressing a preference in the third person ▶ Multiple exercises
6 Writing Agree/Disagree Essays _149	▶ Explanation and common question phrases ▶ How to answer this type of question ▶ Structuring the essay ▶ Analysis of writing by Korean students of English ▶ Essential skills: avoiding the words 'agree' and 'disagree,' writing opposite meanings and sentiments ▶ Multiple exercises

Answers with Explanations _173

Contents STEP 1

Section 1 Essay Skills_13

Unit	Features
1 Planning Your Essay _15	▶ The writing process ▶ Understanding the question ▶ Structuring an essay ▶ Common question types ▶ Generating ideas and creating an outline ▶ Drafting, writing, revising, and editing ▶ Multiple exercises
2 Writing the Introduction _31	▶ Hooks and thesis statements ▶ Analysis of writing by Korean students of English ▶ Essential skills: paraphrasing, thesis statements ▶ Multiple exercises
3 Writing the Essay Body 1 _45	▶ The structure of a body paragraph ▶ Analysis of writing by Korean students of English ▶ Essential skills: topic sentences, concluding sentences ▶ Multiple exercises
4 Writing the Essay Body 2 _65	▶ Expanding and explaining the topic sentence ▶ Validating points or arguments ▶ Analysis of writing by Korean students of English ▶ Essential skills: transitions, validation ▶ Multiple exercises
5 Writing the Conclusion _85	▶ Structuring the conclusion ▶ Final comments ▶ Analysis of writing by Korean students of English ▶ Essential skills: avoiding common conclusion errors, answering the question ▶ Multiple exercises

Contents STEP 1

Section 2 Writing Skills _99

Unit	Features
6 Writing Better Sentences _101	▶ Collocations ▶ Avoiding colloquialisms ▶ Simplicity ▶ Redundancy ▶ Better verbs and nouns ▶ Avoiding clichés and euphemisms ▶ Using fewer words ▶ Conjunctions ▶ Multiple exercises
7 Common Errors _117	▶ Pronouns ▶ The article ▶ Fragments ▶ Run-ons ▶ Comma splices ▶ Multiple exercises
8 Unity and Coherence _131	▶ Transitions ▶ Logical organization ▶ Key noun repetition ▶ Multiple exercises
9 Academic Writing _137	▶ Third person & impersonal writing ▶ Contractions ▶ Plagiarism ▶ Citation ▶ Reference lists and Bibliographies ▶ Multiple exercises

Section 1

Essay Types 1
Cause and Effect | Advantages/Disadvantages | Compare and Contrast

Section 1

Essay Types 1

Unit 1 Writing Cause and Effect Essays

Writing Focus

This type of question asks you to explain why an event, situation or action makes a particular outcome or result occur. The cause (the first action) creates or influences the situation to create the effect (the result / outcome).

> *e.g.* The gap in wealth between the rich and the poor is increasing in many countries. Why is this happening and what are the effects?

So, for this question you would need to explain why the rich/poor gap is growing (the cause), and explain what happens due to the rich/poor gap getting bigger (the effect).

Occasionally, this type of question will also ask you to propose some solutions.

> *e.g.* The gap in wealth between the rich and the poor is increasing in many countries. Why is this happening and what are the effects? Suggest some possible solutions.

— More to Know **Common phrases in a 'cause and effect' question:**

- **What are the reasons and results of…?**
- **Why is this happening and what are the consequences?**
- **Discuss the causes and effects of…**
- **Discuss the causes for this phenomenon.**
- **What causes this and what are the implications?**
- **Explain why this is happening and what the implications are.**

What is a 'cause' and what is an 'effect'?

▶ The cause is what happened (or what is happening), and the effect is the result of that happening. The structure of your sentence can usually be 'cause/effect' or 'effect/cause':

> Cause: When it started raining
> Effect: everybody had to use his or her umbrella.
>
> Effect: Everybody had to use his or her umbrella
> Cause: because it started raining.

▶ There can be more than one effect for a particular cause, or more than one cause for a particular effect:

> Cause: Heavy drinking leads to
> Multiple Effects: various problems such as ❶ liver disease and ❷ obesity.
>
> Effect: Obesity is increasing due to
> Multiple Causes: ❶ eating too much junk food and ❷ not getting enough exercise.

How do I answer this type of question?

▶ You need to analyze the question to make sure you understand the topic. In the following question the topic is that the gap between the rich and the poor is increasing:

The gap in wealth between the rich and the poor is increasing in many countries. Why is this happening and what are the effects?

▶ Then you must choose at least two causes for the increase in the gap between the rich and poor, and show what effects these causes have.

▶ If the question asks for some solutions, it is often easiest to write your ideas for the solutions in a separate paragraph.

▶ You must make sure you clearly show the relationship between the cause and the effect. You can use the following signal words and phrases to show the direct relationship between cause and effect:

Cause and Effect signal words and phrases:			
affects	brings about	causes	consequence of
as a result of	because	results	leads to
creates	effects	produces	reasons
makes	outcome	due to	because of

▶ You should not give an opinion on the topic. If you are asked to propose solutions you should write the solutions without stating your view on the topic:

☺ To help combat obesity, schools should provide more nutritious meals.
☹ I think that school meals are terrible. They do not taste nice and are not healthy. In my opinion the most important thing to do is make school meals better.

How do I structure a 'cause and effect' essay?

There are two main ways to structure a cause and effect essay:

Type 1: 'cause and effect' by 'cause and effect'

Use this type of structure if you need to show the <u>direct relationship</u> between each cause and effect (and if applicable, each solution):

▶ **Introduction** – explain the topic by using a hook and paraphrasing the question. Your thesis statement should list the causes and the effects you will include in your essay
▶ **Body paragraph 1** – cause, and the cause's direct effect 1 (and solution)
▶ **Body paragraph 2** – cause, and the cause's direct effect 2 (and solution)
▶ **Conclusion** – restate the topic and briefly summarize the causes, effects, and if applicable, the proposed solutions.

An example of a direct relationship between a cause and effect is that having healthy teeth is a <u>direct result</u> of brushing your teeth properly:

> The girl had strong, white teeth as a consequence of brushing her teeth after every meal.

Type 2: 'causes paragraph' and 'effects paragraph'

Use this type of structure if you need to explain a topic but <u>do not need to show a direct relationship</u> between each cause and each effect.

- ▶ **Introduction** – explain the topic by using a hook and paraphrasing the question. Your thesis statement should list the causes and the effects you will include in your essay
- ▶ **Body paragraph 1** – causes
- ▶ **Body paragraph 2** – effects
- ▶ (If applicable **Body paragraph 3** – solutions)
- ▶ **Conclusion** – restate the topic and briefly summarize the causes, effects, and if applicable, the proposed solutions.

For instance, there is <u>not such a direct relationship</u> between eating fruit and having healthy teeth, even though fruit is far better for your teeth than candy. Therefore this type of effect (healthy teeth) and cause (eating fruit) is better suited to an essay structure in which there is a paragraph for the causes and a paragraph for the effects.

How do I write the introduction?

- ▶ The opening sentence for this type of essay should provide a hook and some background information on the topic.
- ▶ Write a strong thesis statement that briefly states the causes and effects of the topic. If the question asks you to think of some solutions you must also state your solutions in the thesis statement.

— More to Know **Useful words and phrases for 'cause and effect' introductions:**

- There are several reasons why ... Firstly,
- The (topic) has many causes and implications. (cause) leads to (effect), and (effect) is caused by (cause)
- There are many possible solutions to this problem, such as...

Let's *analyze* an introduction for this type of essay

Q: Discuss the causes and effects of divorce.

(A) Marriage can be the most wonderful part of a person's life, but sadly marriages often go wrong and end with the couple separating. **(B)** Divorce is often caused by a lack of communication between the couple, and frequently couples divorce because of money problems. Divorce can lead to emotional stress and it also results in an increasing number of people living alone.

A This is the opening sentence that provides a hook and some background information.

B This is the thesis statement. It states two causes (lack of communication and money), and it states two effects (stress and living alone).

How do I write the body paragraphs?

▶ If you are writing a 'cause and effect' by 'cause and effect' type structure, you must write only one cause and its effect per paragraph. Make sure the effect is a direct consequence of the cause.

▶ If you are writing a 'causes paragraph' or an 'effects paragraph' you must state all the causes (or all the effects) in a logical order and use an appropriate signal word or phrase between each cause (or each effect).

▶ There must be a clear topic sentence and concluding sentence for each paragraph.

▶ Each cause and effect must be relevant to the topic and clearly linked to the topic.

▶ Appropriate examples can be included, but are not always required. If you have written a detailed explanation of the causes and effects, it is not always necessary to include examples. However, if you have simply stated the cause and/or effect, then you must include examples to validate your point.

▶ You must use appropriate transitions. See the boxes below for useful transition words and phrases.

— More to Know

Useful words and phrases for 'cause and effect' body paragraphs:

Type 1 essays – 'cause and effect' by 'cause and effect'

> Topic sentence phrases:
> - (Cause) leads to/results in (effect)
> - The main consequence of (cause) is (effect)
> - The primary reason that (effect) occurs is due to/because of (cause)
>
> Phrases to introduce the second paragraph:
> - Another cause and effect of (topic) is…
> - (topic) is also caused by…
> - A further result/consequence/outcome/etc. of…

Type 2 essays – a 'causes paragraph' and an 'effects paragraph'

> Topic sentence phrases:
> - There are numerous causes of (topic). Firstly…
> - (cause) and (cause) are the main reasons of (topic)
> - The implications of (topic) are … and …
> - (effect) and (effect) arise as a consequence of (cause)
> - As a consequence of the causes of (topic)…
> - These causes have numerous effects. Firstly,…
> - The results/consequences of this situation are…

Let's *analyze* topic sentences for 'cause and effect' essays

Type 1 – 'cause and effect' by 'cause and effect'

Q: Discuss the causes and effects of divorce.

The primary reason for divorce is a lack of communication between the husband and wife. The effect of not communicating effectively is often an increased level of stress in the household.

> The topic sentence mentions the topic (divorce), the cause (lack of communication), and the effect (stress).

Type 2 – a 'causes paragraph' and an 'effects paragraph'

Q: Discuss the causes and effects of divorce.

Causes:
Money problems and a lack of communication are common factors contributing to couples getting divorced.

> The 'causes' topic sentence mentions two reasons for divorce.

Effects:
As a consequence of divorce, people tend to experience higher stress levels and often live alone.

> The 'effects' topic sentence mentions outcomes of divorce.

How do I write the conclusion?

▶ Use a clear 'conclusion transition.'
▶ The conclusion for this type of essay is very short. You should summarize all the causes and effects you have mentioned (and the solutions if applicable), and link them directly to the topic.

> **Conclusion transitions:**
>
> in conclusion   in summary   on the whole   therefore
> to sum up   in short   for the reasons illustrated

Let's *analyze* a conclusion for this type of essay:

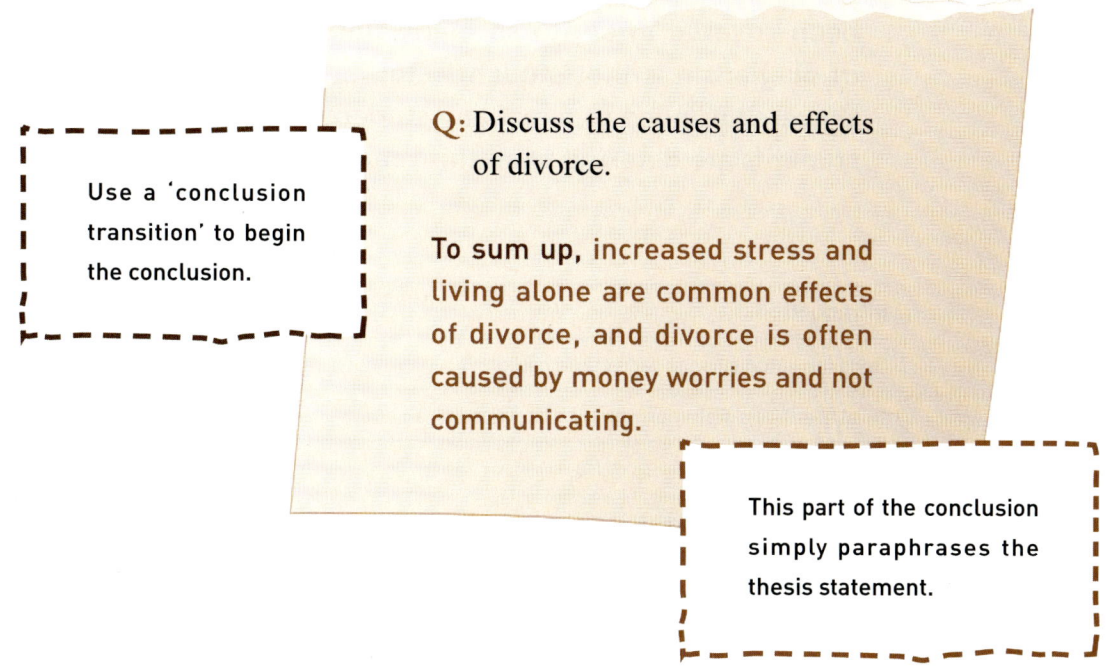

Use a 'conclusion transition' to begin the conclusion.

Q: Discuss the causes and effects of divorce.

To sum up, increased stress and living alone are common effects of divorce, and divorce is often caused by money worries and not communicating.

This part of the conclusion simply paraphrases the thesis statement.

Exercise 1a

The following paragraphs were written in response to this question:

Q: More and more university students are being caught plagiarising others' work. Why is this happening and what are the consequences? Suggest some solutions to combat plagiarism.

1 Use the checklist to evaluate this introduction.

The pressure on students to succeed at university is intense, and therefore it is not surprising that some students try to use every possible method to get the best grades. Plagiarism is increasing because it is becoming harder and harder to be original when most subjects have been covered in depth so many times previously, and an implication of plagiarism is that students stop being able to think for themselves. Universities need to expel any student caught plagiarising so that other students are deterred from this practice.

Introduction	YES	NO
Does the introduction provide some background information and a hook?		
Does the thesis statement clearly state a cause, an effect and a solution?		

2 Use the checklist to evaluate this body paragraph.

> **In terms of solutions to combat plagiarism, universities need to expel anyone caught plagiarising. If a student is expelled from university they cannot commit plagiarism anymore so the problem will disappear.**

Body paragraph	YES	NO
Is there an appropriate transition to begin the paragraph?		
Are there a clear topic sentence and a concluding sentence?		
Is there sufficient explanation or validation of the solution?		

3 Use the checklist to evaluate this conclusion.

> **Universities should expel students caught plagiarising, because the effects of plagiarism are disruptive. Students plagiarise due to the pressure of university study.**

Conclusion	YES	NO
Is there a clear conclusion transition?		
Does it clearly paraphrase the causes, effects and solutions?		

Check your answers with the answer key at the back of the book.

Real Essays

In this section we will review a 'cause and effect' essay written by a Korean student of English.

step 1 Read through the student's essay and highlight parts that could be improved. There is a note section at the end of the essay for you to write your ideas and comments.

Question: In many countries, obesity levels in children are increasing. Explain why this is happening and what the implications are.

Nowadays, increasing number of children suffer from obesity, as their food habits and life style are changing. There are a lot of reasons for this situation, lack of exercise and junk food are significant factors. In this situation children would be damaged from diseases such as diabetes or high blood pressure, and also they can be too weak.

Most children are keen to eat junk food. This is because of the increasing number of commercial food companies which are interested in maximising their profit rather than children's health. The companies try to attract children to eat their food by using some chemical materials such as additives. Children tend to be easily addicted to these junk foods. Moreover, children are becoming quite lazy, as technology and equipment are becoming advanced. These things make children spend their time in front of a computer or the TV, instead of children going outside and doing physical activities.

Lack of exercise and changed food habit could be negative effect on children. If they continue unhealthy food habits, will get some serious diseases, such as diabetes, high blood pressure, or heart disease. In addition, the child who do not likely go outside and spend a lot of time at home has more potential to get depression and have weaker immune system. Therefore, their health will get worse mentally and physically.

In conclusion, these days, the number of children who suffer from obesity crosses the line. We should take care of children's health, together.

Your notes:

....

....

....

....

step 2 Here are some comments made by the marker of this essay. Compare the marker's comments with the items you found.

 Marker's Comments

Question: In many countries, obesity levels in children are increasing. Explain why this is happening and what the implications are.

Nowadays, an increasing number of children suffer from obesity, as their food habits and life style are changing. There are a lot of reasons for this situation,; lack of exercise and junk food are significant factors. In this situation children wcould be damaged from diseases such as diabetes or high blood pressure, and also they can be too weak.

- It is more commonly written as one word 'lifestyle.'

- This is a good thesis statement. It includes both causes of childhood obesity (lack of exercise and junk food) and effects of childhood obesity (illnesses). However, the last point ('can be too weak') is too vague.

Most children are keen to eat junk food. This is because of the increasing number of commercial food companies ~~which~~ that are interested in maximising their profit rather than children's health. The companies try to attract children to eat their food by using some chemical ~~materials~~ ingredients such as additives. Children tend to be easily addicted to these junk foods. Moreover, children are becoming quite lazy, as technology and equipment are becoming advanced. These things make children spend their time in front of a computer or the TV, instead of ~~children~~ going outside and doing physical activities.

A ~~L~~lack of exercise and changed food habits ~~could be~~ have a negative effect on children. If ~~they~~ children continue unhealthy food habits, they will get some serious diseases, such as diabetes, high blood pressure, or heart disease. In addition, ~~the~~ a child who does not ~~likely~~ go outside and spends a lot of time at home has more potential to get depress~~ion~~ed and have a weaker immune system. Therefore, their health will get worse mentally and physically.

In conclusion, these days, the number of children who suffer from obesity ~~crosses the line~~. We should take care of children's health, together.

- Your points should be in the same order as written in the thesis statement.

- By combining this sentence into the previous sentence you can make the cause and effect more obvious: "Children are easily addicted to junk food because of the additives."

- What is equipment? Better as '...equipment such as MP3 players...'

- You do not need to repeat this noun here.

- You are now explaining the effects of the causes. Every cause has an effect, so you need to be direct in your statement.

- Be careful with pronouns. 'They' could refer to the lack of exercise and changed food habits.

- You start this paragraph using 'children' (plural), then switch to 'a child' (singular), then go back to 'their' (plural). Try to be consistent.

- This is not quite the correct way to use this idiom. The question asks why obesity is increasing, it does not ask for your opinion.

- The question asks for the causes and implications, it does not ask for your opinion. Your conclusion should restate the thesis statement.

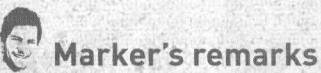

Marker's remarks

Well done – a good essay that lists the causes and effects of the topic well, although perhaps there could be a little more explanation and validation of each point you make.

The conclusion is the weakest part of the essay – try not to use idioms and you must avoid opinions in cause and effect essays.

Your use of English is generally quite good, although you need to be careful with punctuation and the use of pronouns.

step 3 Here is the same question answered by a native-English speaker:

There are two primary reasons why childhood obesity is increasing. Firstly, children's lifestyles are different than in the past, which leads to a more inactive way of living. Secondly, the food children eat these days is often not healthy, and consequently children eat too much fat and sugar.

In the past, children were more active. Instead of getting the bus to school they used to walk. Instead of playing on a computer they used to play outside. Instead of sending text messages to their friends, they used to run to their friend's house. Advances in technology and the way modern society operates contribute to children getting less exercise than children of bygone eras, and therefore nowadays children do not burn off the calories they consume. This trend can be seen particularly clearly in the developed western world, where the last few generations have grown up in an affluent society. The countries with a high standard of living such as the US and the UK have very high child obesity rates because most of the children from these countries have access to the technology and live the lifestyle that stops them getting enough physical activity. It is clear that a lack of exercise causes weight gain.

These days, parents are often too busy to prepare fresh and healthy food for their children. And often parents nowadays do not even know the basics of cooking and nutrition. These two factors mean that children tend to eat too much processed food that has very high fat and sugar levels. Walk down any high street and it is difficult not to see how successful the fast food chains have become over the last few generations. Walk down the aisle of a supermarket and it is easier to find cans and tins and packets of cheap processed food than it is to find cheap, fresh, and nutritious food. Eating too much fat and sugar brings about weight gain, and perpetually eating a poor diet results in obesity.

A lack of exercise due to modern lifestyles, combined with a poor diet high in fat and sugar, are two significant factors in the increasing obesity rates in children.

Exercise 1b

Examine the essay written by the <u>native speaker of English</u> and answer the following questions. See the answer key at the back of the book for explanations.

❶ Circle the 'cause and effect' signal words used by the native speaker in the essay:

affects	brings about	causes	consequence of
as a result of	because	results	leads to
creates	effects	produces	reasons
makes	outcome	due to	because of

❷ List any other 'cause and effect' signal words used in the essay:

....

....

....

❸ Which type of 'cause and effect' essay structure did the native speaker use in the essay?

Type 1 'cause and effect' by 'cause and effect'
Or
Type 2 'causes paragraph' and an 'effects paragraph'

4 Use this checklist to evaluate both body paragraphs of the essay.

	YES	NO
Is there a clear topic sentence in each paragraph?		
Is there a clear concluding sentence in each paragraph?		
Is there sufficient 'expansion and explanation' of the topic sentence?		
Is the order in which the points are made the same as in the 'thesis statement'?		
Is each point adequately validated?		
Is there a clear transition between the two paragraphs?		

5 Does the essay fully answer the question? If it does not fully answer the question, why not?

....

....

....

....

....

....

....

....

....

Essential Skills

Skill A: Knowing the difference between a cause and an effect

Remember, a cause is what happened (or what is happening), and an effect is the result of that happening.

Cause	Effect
More cars on the roads	Longer time to get to work
Oil spill in the ocean	Fish and wildlife die
Lots of demand for goods	Price goes up

Exercise 1c

See the answer key at the back of the book to check your answers.

1 Underline the **cause** and circle the (**effect**) in these pairs:
   e.g. (people being rescued) / <u>a fire in the building</u>

   a. Parents spend less time at home / children who have little respect for elders

   b. unable to sleep properly / drinking too much caffeine

   c. inflation / rising oil prices

   d. lots of practice / winning the game

   e. reading a newspaper every day / increased knowledge of current affairs

   f. being punished / being naughty

2 **Use the transition words you have learned in this unit to make complete sentences using the pairs from Exercise 1c, ❶:**

e.g. As a consequence of a fire in the building, many people needed to be rescued.

a.
....

....

b.
....

....

c.
....

....

d.
....

....

e.
....

....

f.
....

....

Skill B: Linking causes and effects using signal words and phrases

Being able to correctly link causes and effects is a vital skill you need to master in order to effectively show the relationship between a cause and an effect.

Remember that the sentence structure can be 'cause/effect' or 'effect/cause.'

Some examples of words and phrases that signal the cause:

> **Due to ~**
> - Due to overeating, he became fat.
> - He became fat due to overeating.
>
> **As a result of ~**
> - As a result of not drinking, she fainted.
> - She fainted as a result of not drinking.

Some example words and phrases that signal the effect:

> **Leads to ~**
> - Eating excessively leads to weight gain.
>
> **Consequently ~**
> - She did not drink enough water. Consequently, she fainted.

The difference between 'because' and 'because of'

'because' and 'because of' are very useful to show the reason for something, but you must know how to use them correctly:

▶ 'because' must be followed by a complete sentence
▶ 'because of' can be followed by just a noun phrase

Examples using 'because' and 'because of' after an effect:

▶ Structure: **effect** > because > **cause (complete sentence containing a subject and verb)**
  e.g. **People do not get enough sleep** because **they play computer games late at night**.

▶ Structure: **effect** > because of > **cause (noun phrase)**
  e.g. **People do not use public transport** because of **the lack of infrastructure**.

Examples using 'because' and 'because of' at the beginning of a sentence, using a comma after the cause:

▶ Structure: Because > **cause (complete sentence containing a subject and verb)** > comma > **effect**
  e.g. Because **people play computer games late at night**, **they do not get enough sleep**.

▶ Structure: Because of > **cause (noun phrase)** > comma > **effect**
  e.g. Because of **the lack of infrastructure**, **people do not use public transport**.

Exercise 1d

1 Insert either 'because' or 'because of' in the sentences.

a. Growing up in the countryside is good _____ the clean air.
b. _____ young people are not interested in traditional crafts, many skills are being lost.
c. _____ the increase in greenhouse gases, the climate is getting warmer.

d. Many people move to cities _____ there are more job opportunities.

e. Mountain climbing is considered a great hobby _____ the views from the top are amazing.

2 Rewrite the following sentences to put 'because' or 'because of' at the beginning of the sentence:

a. Factories should pay more taxes because they pollute the environment.

....

b. People like to live by the sea because of the fresh air.

....

c. Tables of information are hard to describe because there is too much data.

....

3 Rewrite the following sentences to put 'because' or 'because of' after the effect:

a. Because many people moved there, the country became very powerful.

....

b. Because of deforestation, many birds have lost their natural habitats.

....

c. Because of the change in the tax law, many poor people will have even more financial hardship.

....

Further Practice

Write a _complete essay_ for each of these questions. Once you have completed your essays, use this checklist to evaluate your writing.

Introduction	YES	NO
Does the introduction provide some background information and a hook?		
Does the thesis statement clearly state causes, effects and if applicable, a solution?		
Body paragraphs	**YES**	**NO**
Is there a clear topic sentence in each paragraph?		
Is there a clear concluding sentence in each paragraph?		
Is there sufficient 'expansion and explanation' of the topic sentence?		
Are the paragraphs correctly written considering the structure type (type 1 or type 2)?		
Is each point adequately validated?		
Is there a clear transition between the two paragraphs?		
Conclusion	**YES**	**NO**
Is there a clear conclusion transition?		
Does it clearly paraphrase the causes, effects and solutions?		

1 In general, people are living for longer nowadays. Discuss the causes and effects of this phenomenon.

Ideas box:

Cause	
Effects	

2 What are the causes and effects of noise pollution? Suggest some ways to minimize noise pollution.

Ideas box:

Causes	
Effects	
Solutions	

....

....

....

....

....

....

....

....

....

....

....

....

Unit 2: Writing Advantages/Disadvantages Essays

Writing Focus

This type of question asks you to write about the advantages and disadvantages of a specific topic.

> *e.g.* Compare the advantages and disadvantages of building a new factory in your community. Use specific details in your discussion.

— More to Know

Common phrases in an 'advantages/disadvantages' question:

- What are the advantages and disadvantages of...?
- **Discuss both the advantages and disadvantages of...**
- **Compare the advantages and disadvantages of...**

How do I answer this type of question?
▸ An 'advantage/disadvantage' question does not ask for your opinion or preference. Make sure that you only state advantages and disadvantages and that you do not express a preference or opinion.

▸ Usually, you will need to give two or three advantages and the same amount of disadvantages. Very occasionally the question specifically asks for 'the advantage and disadvantage,' so you would only need to make one point for each:

> Discuss the advantage and disadvantage of giving aid to poor countries.

How do I structure an 'advantages/disadvantages' essay?
▸ **Introduction**
▸ **Body paragraph 1** - advantages
▸ **Body paragraph 2** - disadvantages
▸ **Conclusion**

How do I write the introduction?
▸ The opening sentence for this type of essay should provide a hook and some background information on the topic.

▸ There is no thesis statement in this type of essay, because you are not giving an opinion or making a claim. Instead, you need to write an 'essay statement.' An essay statement contains the advantages and disadvantages, but does not include an opinion or preference.

An example of an 'essay statement':

> The advantages of a new factory in my community are that it will create new jobs and will benefit local businesses. Conversely, it will cause heavy traffic in the area and will increase pollution levels.

▸ There should be an equal number of advantages and disadvantages.

— More to Know

Useful words and phrases for advantage/disadvantage introductions:

- A/The main/major/primary advantage/disadvantage of... is...
- The advantages/disadvantages of... are...
- ...has the following advantages/disadvantages. Firstly...
- Conversely/However/On the other hand there are also many/some advantages/disadvantages of..., such as...
- There are both benefits and drawbacks...

Let's *analyze* an introduction for this type of essay

Q: Discuss the advantage and disadvantage of giving aid to poor countries.

(A)There are hundreds of countries in the world, and they are not all the same. (B)Some countries are wealthy enough to be able to assist poorer ones, while other countries struggle to provide even the most basic living standards to its people. (C)A major advantage of giving aid to less fortunate countries is that it can help the poorer country supply crucial necessities, such as food and clean water, to its citizens. However, a significant drawback is that the poorer country may become too reliant on the aid.

A This is the hook. It makes a statement that makes the reader wonder what the essay is about.

B This is the opening sentence. It has a 'hook' to get the reader's attention, and provides background information and general discussion of the topic.

C This is the essay statement. Because the question asks for 'the advantage and disadvantage,' the essay statement only provides one advantage and one disadvantage.

How do I write the body paragraphs?

▶ Write the first paragraph to explain the advantage(s) of the topic, and write the second paragraph to explain the disadvantage(s).

▶ There must be a clear topic sentence for each paragraph.

▶ There should be an equal number of advantages and disadvantages.

▶ Each advantage and each disadvantage must be supported by appropriate reasons and logic, but it is not always necessary to include examples.

▶ Use appropriate 'addition transitions' between the points within each paragraph.

▶ You must use an appropriate transition between the two paragraphs. A 'disadvantage' is a contrast to an 'advantage,' so use a 'contrast transition' to begin the second paragraph.

— More to Know

Useful words and phrases for advantage/disadvantage body paragraphs:

Topic sentence phrases:
- One of the primary/main/major advantages/disadvantages of... is that...
- ...that it would increase/decrease/cause/harm/improve/contribute...
- The first advantage/disadvantage of...

'Addition' transition words for use within each paragraph:

equally important	firstly (secondly, etc.)	furthermore	in addition
also	another	moreover	next
lastly	finally		

'Contrast transition' words for use between paragraph 1 and paragraph 2:

although	despite	even though	however
in contrast	in spite of	nevertheless	on the contrary
on the other hand	but	conversely	

Let's *analyze* a topic sentence for this type of essay

Q: Discuss the advantage and disadvantage of giving aid to poor countries.

(A) On the other hand, **(B)** giving aid to poor countries can actually hinder the country from becoming more independent.

> **A** Use a 'contrast transition' to begin the second paragraph.

> **B** The topic sentence must clearly state the actual disadvantage(s) you will discuss in the paragraph.

How do I write the conclusion?

▶ Use a clear 'conclusion transition.'

▶ The conclusion should just restate the advantage(s) or disadvantage(s) you have mentioned in the essay statement.

▶ It is very important not to give an opinion or preference in your conclusion.

— More to Know

Useful words and phrases for advantage/disadvantage conclusions:

<u>Conclusion transitions:</u>

in conclusion	in summary	on the whole	therefore
to sum up	in short	for the reasons illustrated	

47

Let's *analyze* a conclusion for this type of essay:

Q: Discuss the advantage and disadvantage of giving aid to poor countries.

ⒶIn conclusion, Ⓑassisting poor countries by providing aid can be beneficial as it helps the poor country to adequately care for its citizens. However, it can also lengthen the time it takes for a poor country to become self-reliant.

Ⓐ Use a 'conclusion transition' to begin the conclusion.

Ⓑ Paraphrase the 'essay statement.' Do not add any preference or opinion.

Exercise 2a

❶ Use the checklist to evaluate this introduction.

> Everybody wants a convenient life. From taking the children to school to going shopping to visiting relatives, people use their cars more and more these days. Cars can take a person exactly where the person wants to go, and cars are available for use at a moment's notice. Conversely, cars can be expensive and driving is not always pleasurable. Therefore, people should make more use of public transport.

Introduction	YES	NO
Is there an opening sentence that includes a 'hook'?		
Is there an essay statement rather than a thesis statement?		
Is there an equal number of advantages and disadvantages?		
Have opinions and preferences been omitted?		

2 Use the checklist to evaluate this body paragraph.

> Firstly, a car needs to be serviced regularly. Therefore, it costs a lot to keep the car working properly. Driving can be stressful. For example, being caught in a traffic jam can be quite traumatic. Cars can be costly to maintain and driving a car is not always a pleasant experience.

Body paragraph	YES	NO
Are there a clear topic sentence and a concluding sentence?		
Are there clear transitions between each of the disadvantages?		

3 Use the checklist to evaluate this conclusion.

> To sum up, an advantage of owning a car is that it is immediately available for use. However, car ownership can be costly, and driving can be stressful.

Conclusion	YES	NO
Is there a clear conclusion transition?		
Does it paraphrase the essay statement?		
Have opinions and preferences been omitted?		

Check your answers with the answer key at the back of the book.

Real Essays

In this section we will review an 'advantages/disadvantages' essay written by a Korean student of English.

 **step 1** Read through the student's essay and highlight parts that could be improved. There is a note section at the end of the essay for you to write your ideas and comments.

Question: Compare the advantages and disadvantages of establishing a new university in a community. Use specific details in your discussion.

People Sometimes think that good or bad buildings give to their quality of community. A new university in my community has the following main the advantage and main disadvantage.
 The main advantage is that it can help to improve quality of community's education. My community think that education is important. Because With its geographical disadvantage and a lack of natural resources, my community put strong emphasis on education in order to harvest prominent human resources. If the new university build in my community, it gives to develop education activity. For instance, other community has good university. Many students try to admission this university, and their can develop to education. Building a New university affect to develop education in community.
 The main disadvantage is that it is too stressful for community people. Our community will crowded and complex even though building a new university gives a lot of benefits. Many people and a lot of cars come to a university, It caused noise and busy community. Living a good community is important.

Your notes:

....

....

step 2

Here are some comments made by the marker of this essay. Compare the marker's comments with the items you found.

Marker's Comments

Question: Compare the advantages and disadvantages of establishing a new university in a community. Use specific details in your discussion.

People Ssometimes think that good or bad ~~buildings~~ ~~give to their~~ improve the quality of their community. A new university in my community has the following ~~main the~~ advantage and main disadvantage.

The main advantage is that it can help to improve the quality of my community's education. My community thinks that education is important. Because ~~With its~~ it has a geographical disadvantage and a lack of natural resources, my community puts strong emphasis on education ~~in order to~~ harvest prominent human resources. If ~~the~~ a new university ~~build~~ were built in my community, it ~~gives to~~ would develop education activity. For instance, another community has a good university. Many students try to get admission to this university, and their can develop to education. Building a ~~N~~new university affects ~~the~~ to development of education in a community.

The main disadvantage is that it is too stressful for ~~community~~ people in the community. ~~Our~~ My community will be crowded and complex even though building a new university gives a lot of benefits. Many people and a lot of cars come to a university, ~~It~~ which caused noise and a busy community. Living in a good community is important.

- The question is specifically about a university. Try to find a more suitable synonym.

- This could be improved by using some synonyms and by stating the actual advantages/disadvantages. And very importantly the questions asks for advantages and disadvantages, therefore you cannot just discuss one of each.

- In your topic sentence it is better to write the noun rather than use a pronoun.

- 'of education in my community' and 'People in my community' are the correct way to word these phrases. A 'community' cannot 'think' – the people do.

- In this context this means 'educate famous or important people.' Is this what you mean?

- The meaning here is not clear and the validation is a little weak.

- This is OK, but it is the identical structure to how you started the first body paragraph. A 'contrast transition' would be better.

- Specify what 'it' is in your topic sentence.

- Be consistent throughout your essay.

- This type of phrase is OK in the topic sentence to introduce the disadvantage, but you should only write about disadvantages in the rest of the paragraph.

- Do not include opinions in this type of essay.

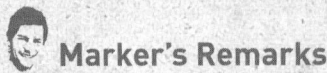 Marker's Remarks

You have tried to structure the essay correctly, although there should be a brief conclusion. Importantly, the question asks you to compare the advantages and disadvantages, so you need to include at least two advantages and two disadvantages.

In your body paragraphs make sure that each paragraph has a clear topic sentence and a clear concluding sentence.

Within the first body paragraph you have included a general statement and an example, but the logic of the argument is not particularly clear. I think you are trying to say that your community would benefit because people within the community would receive a better education.

You should try to write approximately the same amount for each body paragraph. You have written far more for the advantage than for the disadvantage.

step 3 Here is the same question answered by a native-English speaker:

Most people would like the community in which they live to be as pleasant and prosperous as possible. My own neighbourhood does not have any higher education establishments, and if a new university were to be built it would certainly affect the local population. A new university would create new jobs, give more educational opportunities to local residents, and bring some much-needed culture to the community. Conversely, it would increase traffic in the area, destroy some of the natural habitat, and strain the local services.

A new university would bring many improvements to my district.
One of the primary benefits would be the jobs it would create. A university requires an array of workers from administrators to cleaners, and local inhabitants would likely fill these positions. Furthermore, a new university would provide local educational facilities to the community's residents. High-school graduates who currently have to travel long distances to enter higher education would have a closer option, and most universities provide adult and evening classes for the local populace. The third main advantage would be the new cultural opportunities that would be available to locals. A higher education facility often hosts concerts, plays and sporting events for instance.
My community would certainly benefit from these consequences of a new university being built.

On the other hand, a new university in my area would also have some significant drawbacks.
The road infrastructure in my neighbourhood is underdeveloped, so a new university would only add to the existing traffic chaos and make parking even more difficult. Another negative aspect would be the destruction of the natural environment in order to build the campus. There are precious few parks and open spaces left in my community, and a new university could potentially remove a space that is currently enjoyed and used by the local people. Lastly, public services such as buses and health care would likely come under increased burden due to the increase in the local population.
There would definitely be some problems associated with a new university in my community.

In conclusion, a new university would improve my local community by providing employment, cultural and educational opportunities. However, it would lead to traffic and public service problems, and would diminish the amount of recreational land available to local residents.

Exercise 2b

Examine the essay written by the <u>native speaker of English</u> and answer the following questions. See the answer key at the back of the book for explanations.

❶ What synonyms and/or alternative phrases were used for the following words?

advantages: ....

community: ....

disadvantages: ....

university: ....

residents: ....

❷ List the transition words and transition phrases used in the essay.

....

....

....

❸ What is wrong with this essay?

....

....

....

Essential Skills

Skill A: Writing the 'essay statement' part of the introduction

List your advantages and disadvantages:

▶ Make sure you have the same number of advantages as disadvantages (usually 2 or 3 points for each).

▶ Prioritize the order of importance and use this order for your essay statement and the body text:

- If you state A, B, C in the essay statement, the order that these points appear in the body text should also be A, B, C.

Let's look at an example of an 'essay statement':

Q: Compare the advantages and disadvantages of establishing a new factory in your community. Use specific details in your discussion.

Ideas box:

Advantages	Priority	Disadvantages	Priority
Create jobs	❶	Traffic	②
Benefit local business	❷	Noise	③
Bring more investment	❸	Pollution	①

Essay statement part of the introduction:
My neighbourhood would benefit from a new factory as the factory would ❶create jobs, ❷provide local businesses with more trading opportunities, and ❸attract investment into the area. However, it would also ①increase local pollution levels, ②cause more traffic chaos, and ③contribute to higher noise levels.

Exercise 2c

Prioritize these advantages and disadvantages, and then write an 'essay statement.' See the answer key at the back of the book for examples.

> Q: Compare the advantages and disadvantages of solar energy.

Ideas box:

Advantages	Priority	Disadvantages	Priority
Low maintenance		High initial cost	
Low ongoing costs		Requires lots of sun	
Environmentally friendly		No energy made at night	

Essay statement of the introduction:

....

....

....

....

....

....

....

....

Q: Compare the advantages and disadvantages of wearing a school uniform.

Ideas box:

Advantages	Priority	Disadvantages	Priority
Better school spirit		Lack of individuality	
Reduces conflict		Often expensive	
Promotes discipline		Only worn at school	

Essay statement of the introduction:

....

....

....

....

....

....

....

....

....

....

Skill B: Do not give an opinion or preference

▶ It is very important not to give an opinion or preference in the 'essay statement' of an advantage/disadvantage essay.

Let's *look at* an example of an introduction that contains an opinion:

Q: Compare the advantages and disadvantages of using a computer.

These days, computers are used for everything. From shopping to games to homework, our lives are made more convenient because of computers. However, the disadvantages of computers far outweigh the advantages; people become anti-social and they harm their eyesight.

> This is a thesis statement; it gives the writer's opinion that the disadvantages 'far outweigh' the advantages.

Exercise 2d

Rewrite the following introductions:

- First, paraphrase or alter the opening sentence into your own words.
- Then, rewrite the essay statement by removing the opinion or preference.

Example answers are in the answers section at the back of the book.

> Q: Compare the advantages and disadvantages of living in a big city.
>
> More and more people choose to move to the city these days. Traditional ways to earn money, such as farming, are increasingly disappearing as the world becomes more technology orientated. Living in a big city is great because it is convenient and easy to make friends, while living in the countryside is not so good because there are a lack of facilities and fewer opportunities.

Paraphrase or alternative of the opening sentence	
New essay statement with no opinion or preference	

2

Q: Compare the advantage and disadvantage of using nuclear power.

The world's fossil fuels are finite and human's consumption of power continues to increase. One alternative energy source that is a possible solution to this problem is nuclear power. Although nuclear power is relatively cheap, it is extremely dangerous and there are problems with radioactive waste storage.

Paraphrase or alternative of the opening sentence	
New essay statement with no opinion or preference	

Further Practice

Write a complete essay for each of these questions. Once you have completed your essays, use this checklist to evaluate your writing.

Introduction	YES	NO
Is there an opening sentence that includes a 'hook'?		
Is there an essay statement rather than a thesis statement?		
Is there an equal number of advantages and disadvantages?		
Have I made sure there is no opinion or preference?		
Body paragraphs	**YES**	**NO**
Are there clear topic and concluding sentences?		
Have I mentioned each point in the same order as they are stated in the introduction?		
Is there sufficient support for each advantage and each disadvantage?		
Are there clear transitions between each of the advantages?		
Are there clear transitions between each of the disadvantages?		
Is there a clear contrast transition between the advantages and the disadvantages paragraphs?		
Conclusion	**YES**	**NO**
Have I included a clear conclusion transition?		
Have I paraphrased my essay statement?		
Have I made sure there is no opinion or preference?		

1 **Compare the advantages and disadvantages of being famous.**

Ideas box:

Advantages	Priority	Disadvantages	Priority

2 Compare the advantages and disadvantages of having a part-time job while you are studying.

Ideas box:

Advantages	Priority	Disadvantages	Priority

....

....

....

....

....

....

....

....

....

....

....

....

....

Unit 3 Writing Compare and Contrast Essays

Writing Focus

To compare means to find similarities, while to contrast means to find differences. Therefore, there are three possible questions for this type of essay:

1. To compare two (or more) things

> *e.g.* Compare poetry to science fiction.

To answer this question you emphasize the similarities in the topic. You should not emphasize the differences:

> Poetry and science fiction, although seemingly very different, actually share lots of similarities. Both genres require skilful use of language, and both can be devices for conveying deeper meaning and important messages.

2. To contrast two (or more) things

> *e.g.* Contrast poetry to science fiction.

To answer this question you emphasize the differences in the topic. You should not emphasize the similarities:

> While poetry and science fiction are both types of writing, they are completely different. Poetry is often short and uses techniques such as rhyming and metaphor, while science fiction is usually a long novel that tells a captivating story.

3. To compare and contrast two (or more) things

> *e.g.* Compare and contrast poetry to science fiction.

To answer this question you ==show the similarities and the differences== in the topic:

> Poetry and science fiction are similar in some aspects yet different in others. They both require a clever use of language, but poetry tends to be quite short while science fiction is usually a long novel.

— More to Know

Common phrases in a 'compare and contrast' question:

- Compare these two...
- Compare this with/to...
- Compare X with/to Y
- Compare and contrast X with/to Y
- Contrast...
- What are the similarities and differences...?

How do I answer this type of question?

▸ You must study the question carefully and make sure you answer appropriately. Is it a comparison, a contrast, or both?

▸ You must choose the most relevant and important items about the topic to compare and/or contrast. Your reader must not wonder 'why you are comparing or contrasting these items.'

▸ You must choose the most appropriate structure for your essay. See the next section 'How do I structure...?'

▸ You need to use clear signal words to show your reader whether you are comparing or contrasting.

— More to Know

Compare and contrast signal words and phrases:

To compare:			
in a similar way	similarly	likewise	also
in the same manner			
To contrast:			
although	despite	even though	however
in contrast	in spite of	nevertheless	on the contrary
on the other hand	but	conversely	

▸ You must make sure you include at least two items to compare, or two items to contrast, or two items to compare and contrast.

▸ Try to avoid writing a direct opinion. This type of essay is not asking for your opinion; it is asking you to objectively compare and/or contrast aspects of the topic.

How do I structure a 'compare and contrast' essay?

There are two main ways to structure a 'compare and contrast' essay:

Type 1: 'point by point'
In this type of structure you compare (or contrast) an item of similarity (or difference) per paragraph. You can use this type of structure if you have to just compare OR just contrast, but not to 'compare and contrast'.

- **Introduction** – your thesis statement should clearly show the topic, the items you will describe about the topic, and whether you are comparing or contrasting
- **Body paragraph 1** – first similarity (or difference)
- **Body paragraph 2** – second similarity (or difference)
- **Conclusion** – restate the topic and briefly summarise the comparisons (or contrasts).

For example, body paragraph 1 could discuss that poetry and science fiction are similar in the skilful use of language, and body paragraph 2 could discuss how both poetry and science fiction can contain hidden meanings and messages.

Type 2: 'comparison paragraph' and 'contrast paragraph'
In this type of structure you write the similarities in one paragraph, and the differences in another paragraph.
Use this type of structure if you need to compare AND contrast.

- **Introduction** – your thesis statement should clearly show the topic, the items you will describe about the topic, and that you are comparing and contrasting
- **Body paragraph 1** – compare the similarities
- **Body paragraph 2** – contrast the differences
- **Conclusion** – your conclusion must state the topic and an overview of whether the topic is more suited to comparison or contrast.

For instance, body paragraph 1 could state the poetry and science fiction are similar in that they both use skilful language and have hidden meaning. Body paragraph 2 could state that poetry and science fiction are different in terms of length and composition style. The conclusion needs to make a comment about the topic in terms of whether there are more similarities or more differences. In this case it could say that, "overall, poetry and science fiction share more similarities than differences". However, avoid giving your direct personal opinion (i.e. you should not write, "Overall, poetry is better than science fiction.").

How do I write the introduction?

▶ You should write a hook, although it is not always necessary to write too much background information for this type of essay.

▶ Your thesis statement should clearly show the topic, the items you will describe about the topic, and whether you are comparing, or contrasting, or comparing and contrasting

— More to Know

Common phrases in a 'compare and contrast' introduction:

- **Although it may seem that... and... are very similar/different, actually...**
- **(topic) has/have many common traits. Firstly,...**
- **(topic) has/have very few analogous items. Firstly,...**
- **... and ... alike/unalike in that...**
- **(topic) can be both compared and contrasted. They are the same because... and..., yet they are different due to... and...**

Let's *analyze* an introduction for this type of essay:

Q: Compare and contrast the contribution of artists and scientists to society.

(A) Art versus science is an age-old question. **(B)** The contribution to society from artists and scientists share some similarities and some differences. They can be compared in that they both contribute to making people's lives more enjoyable and stress-free. On the other hand, artists generally only contribute to a person's mental well-being, whereas the work of scientists can literally save thousands of lives.

A There is a very short hook in this introduction. It is not always necessary to write background information for a 'compare and contrast' essay.

B This is the thesis statement. It clearly states the topic (contribution to society of artists and scientists), it tells the reader that the essay will compare and contrast, and it lists the items of similarity and difference.

How do I write the body paragraphs?

▶ If you are writing a 'point by point' type structure, you must write only one point per paragraph. Compare the main similarity (or contrast the difference) in the first paragraph, and the second similarity (or difference) in the second paragraph.

▶ If you are writing a 'comparison paragraph' and an 'contrast paragraph' you must state all the similarities together in one paragraph and all the differences in the second paragraph.

▶ There must be a clear topic sentence and concluding sentence for each paragraph.

▶ Each similarity or difference must be important and precise. The reader must be able to understand why you have chosen to compare or contrast a particular aspect of the topic.

▶ Appropriate examples should be included to validate your comparisons and contrasts.

▶ You must use appropriate transitions.

— More to Know

Useful words and phrases for 'compare and contrast' body paragraphs:

Type 1 essays - 'point by point'

Topic sentence phrases:
- … and … are similar/disparate in that…
- The main likeness/difference …
- The primary reason that … and … are connected/dissimilar is that…

Phrases to introduce the second paragraph:
- Another similarity/difference of (topic) is…
- Likewise, … is another item in common.
- A further similarity/contrast is …

Type 2 essays – a 'comparison paragraph' and a 'contrast paragraph'

Topic sentence phrases:
- There are many common attributes of …. and …. Firstly…
- In contrast, there are also many differences between …. and ….

- … and … are surprisingly similar in many ways. Firstly,…
- On the other hand, the two topics are quite different in many regards.

- Although not immediately apparent, …. and … share much in common
- However, …. and …. also display unique characteristics

Let's *analyze* topic sentences for this type of essay:

Type 1 - 'point by point'

> **Q:** Contrast being rich to being famous
>
> One key difference between being rich and being famous is that having fame does not necessarily mean having wealth.

The topic sentence only mentions one point, and emphasizes a difference.

Type 2 - a 'comparison paragraph' and a 'contrast paragraph'

> **Q:** Compare and contrast being rich to being famous.
>
> On the other hand, being rich does not necessarily mean a person will be recognised in the street, and being famous does not necessarily mean having wealth.

Use a contrast transition to begin the second paragraph. The writer has found two differences between being rich and being famous (recognition and wealth), but has presented them from different viewpoints (the first statement contrasts being rich to being famous, the second contrasts being famous to being rich).

How do I write the conclusion?

▸ Use a clear 'conclusion transition.'
▸ The conclusion for this type of essay should state the topic, the items of similarity and/or difference, and a brief statement about the relationship between the topic and the items you have used.
▸ It should not contain your personal opinion.

— More to Know **Conclusion transitions:**

in conclusion	in summary	on the whole
therefore	to sum up	in short
for the reasons illustrated		

Let's *analyze* a conclusion for this type of essay:

Q: Compare and contrast living in a house to living in an apartment.

^AAs illustrated, ^Bthere are both similarities and differences between living in a house and living in an apartment. ^CThey are the same in that they both provide the basic facilities needed to live; yet they are different in terms of convenience. ^DOverall, apartments and houses have stronger similarities than differences.

A Use a 'conclusion transition' to begin the conclusion.

B This part restates the topic of the question.

C This part restates the points used in the comparison / contrast. (Note that you would usually try to write two of each.)

D This statement shows the writer's opinion that there are more similarities than differences, but it does not give a direct preference or opinion on which is better.

Exercise 3a

The following paragraphs were written in response to this question:

> **Q:** Contrast traveling by bus with traveling using your own car.

1 Use the checklist to evaluate this introduction.

> **Traveling by bus is very different to traveling by car. Firstly, a bus does not go to exactly the right place, whereas a car can park directly outside the destination. Secondly, a bus has a set timetable while a person can use his or her car whenever they wish.**

Introduction	YES	NO
Does the introduction include a hook?		
Does the thesis statement state the topic, the items to be described about the topic, and is it clear whether the essay is a comparison, a contrast, or both?		

2 Use the checklist to evaluate this body paragraph.

> **Another major difference between using a bus or a car is convenience. A person can use his or her car any time they wish whereas a bus only runs at certain times. If a person needs to get somewhere in a hurry it might not be convenient to have to wait for the bus to arrive, whereas if the person has a car he or she can start the journey immediately. An example could be needing to get to the doctors or hospital quickly – a car could potentially get a person there in the same time the person would have to wait just for the bus to arrive. A big contrast between traveling by bus and car is how convenient they are.**

Body paragraph	YES	NO
Is there an appropriate transition to begin the paragraph?		
Is there a clear topic sentence and is there a concluding sentence?		
Is there sufficient explanation and is there sufficient validation?		

3 **Use the checklist to evaluate this conclusion.**

> In summary, there are many differences between using a car and traveling by bus. Using a car is more convenient in terms of both getting to the exact destination and being able to begin a journey whenever required.

Conclusion	YES	NO
Is there a clear conclusion transition?		
Does it state the topic and the items of difference?		

Check your answers with the answer key at the back of the book.

Real Essays

In this section we will review a 'compare and contrast' essay written by a Korean student of English.

 Read through the student's essay and highlight parts that could be improved. There is a note section at the end of the essay for you to write your ideas and comments.

Question: Compare and contrast taking difficult classes at university to taking easier classes.

In Korea, many students enter university, and they take the classes. There are challenging and difficult courses and easier classes. Easier classes can build confidence, stop stress and can get high grade without much effort. Harder classes can also boost a person's confidence, but is different because much effort is required.

First of all easier classes, it is easy to understand the lecture. The lecture is not difficult, so I can get a lot of confidence. However, if I get challenging and difficult classes, I can't understand it well, so I get a lot of stress. Last year, I took a physics class and I could understand it very well because it was not too difficult and I was interested in physics. However, when I took a biology class, I couldn't understand it very well because I wasn't interested in biology and it was too difficult for me to understand. Easier classes are easier than difficult classes but they are better to study because I can understand much better.

Moreover, I spend less time on studying if I take easier classes. Taking an easier class makes me to spend less time because I can understand it well. Then I have more free time and I can enjoy my hobby or leisure time or can learn some useful skills on the free time. If I take challenging and difficult class I have to spend more time on studying and get a lot of stress.

But I do well in a harder class I will also get lots of confidence. For example, if Korean take courses about Korea like Korean culture, they know a lot about it, therefore they can spend less time on studying and do another things.

In sum, easier classes and harder classes are the same in that can get confidence, but different in the amount of effort I have to do.

Your notes:

 **step 2** Here are some comments made by the marker of this essay. Compare the marker's comments with the items you found.

 Marker's Comments

Question: Compare and contrast taking difficult classes at university to taking easier classes.

In Korea, many students enter university, and they take ~~the~~ classes. There are challenging and difficult courses and easier classes. Easier classes can build confidence, stop stress, and ~~a person can get~~ high grades without much effort. Harder classes can also boost a person's confidence, but ~~is~~ are different because much effort is required.

First of all, in easier classes, it is easy to understand the lecture. The lecture is not difficult, so I can get a lot of confidence. However, if I get challenging and difficult classes, I ~~can't~~ cannot understand ~~it~~ them well, so I get a lot of stress. Last year, I took a physics class and I ~~could understand~~ understood it very well because it was not too difficult and I was interested in physics. However, when I took a biology class, I ~~couldn't~~ could not understand it very well because I ~~wasn't~~ was not interested in biology and it was too difficult ~~for me to understand~~. Easier classes are easier than difficult classes but they are better to study because I can understand them much better.

- Perhaps better to combine the first two sentences. "Korean university students are faced with the decision of whether to take easy or difficult classes."
- More common as '...a great deal of effort...'
- Try to write in the third person or impersonally.
- You need to explain why you get confidence. "By understanding and doing well in a class a person becomes more confident in their ability and will continue to enjoy the class."
- This is redundant. You have already stated that you could not understand the class.
- This is an obvious statement that does not add anything to the reader's knowledge.
- Try to avoid giving direct opinions in a compare and contrast essay.

Moreover, I spend less time on studying if I take easier classes. Taking an easier class makes me to spend less time studying because I can understand it the lesson content well. Then I have more free time and I can enjoy my hobby or leisure time or can learn some useful skills on the free time. If I take challenging and difficult class I have to spend more time on studying and get a lot of stress. But if I do well in a harder class I will also get lots of confidence. For example, if a Korean student takes courses about Korea, like Korean culture, they he or she probably already knows a lot about it, therefore they he or she can spend less time on studying and do another things.

In sum, easier classes and harder classes are the same in that a person can get confidence, but are different in the amount of effort I have to do.

- 'enables' would be a slightly better word choice here, and you need to add 'studying' in this sentence to explain exactly what you mean.
- Better to be specific here.
- A bit redundant—you have already stated 'free time' and 'leisure time.'
- A contrast transition would aid the flow of the passage.
- Try to avoid starting sentences with conjunctions. This passage would be better as, "On the other hand, a harder class requires longer study time and can cause stress. A harder class can, however, give a person confidence if he or she does well."
- Here 'another' would mean 'one more of the same thing.' 'other' means 'something different' in this context, so is better.

 **Marker's Remarks**

Generally the English is understandable and well written. However, it is better if you can write this type of essay in the third person or in an impersonal style rather than use the first person, and you must avoid using contractions.

Also, in a compare and contrast essay try to avoid writing very direct opinions; this type of essay is not asking for your opinion.

Very importantly, you have concentrated far more on the contrasts than on the comparisons. Think about the structure of your essay. The question asks you to compare and contrast, so it would be easier to write a comparison paragraph listing all the similarities, and a contrast paragraph that lists the differences.

The logic of your arguments is sound, although the presentation is a little bit disjointed. For instance, in the first body paragraph you expand the point about understanding/not understanding, but you relate this to liking/not liking the subject as much as the difficulty level. You also do not relate it directly to your point about confidence.

step 3 Here is the same question answered by a native-English speaker:

University life can shape one's future, so it is imperative that students get the most out of their time at university. For some students, one decision they have to make is whether to take easy or demanding classes. Easy and hard lessons are similar in that students can either pass or fail, students have to submit their work on time, and take exams. Yet there are also differences. A hard class might provide more satisfaction upon completion, whereas a straightforward class might allow a student to do extra-curricular activities.

In terms of similarities, uncomplicated and arduous classes both require the student to regularly attend lectures, to submit coursework in a timely and acceptable manner, and most courses require students to take exams. Accordingly, at the end of the year a student will either pass or fail the course irrespective of its difficulty level.

On the other hand, there are some important distinctions between the two types of classes. Firstly, if a learner successfully passes a challenging course he or she will feel an enormous amount of pride and satisfaction. Conversely, if a student has taken an easy program then he or she may not be so fulfilled. Secondly, hard classes will probably require more study time than an easy class, which means the undergraduate will have less free time. And although coursework is extremely important at university, a person can learn a great many other skills if he or she actively participates in many extra-curricular activities.

In conclusion, the disparities outweigh the similarities between taking easy and challenging classes, and it is preferable for students to take more rigorous lessons in order to get a good job after leaving university.

Exercise 3b

Examine the essay written by the <u>native speaker of English</u> and answer the following questions. See the answer key at the back of the book for explanations.

1 What synonyms and/or alternative phrases were used for the following words:

easy :
....

difficult:
....

class:
....

student:
....

differences:
....

2 Which type of 'compare and contrast' essay structure did the native speaker use in the essay?

Type 1 – 'point by point'
Or
Type 2 – 'comparison paragraph' and 'contrast paragraph'

85

3 Use this checklist to evaluate both body paragraphs of the essay.

	YES	NO
Is there a clear topic sentence in each paragraph?		
Is there a clear concluding sentence in each paragraph?		
Is there sufficient 'expansion and explanation' of the topic sentence?		
Is the order in which the points are made the same as in the 'thesis statement'?		
Is each point adequately validated?		
Is there a clear transition between the two paragraphs?		

4 What is wrong with the conclusion in the essay?

....

....

....

....

Essential Skills

Skill A: 'Compare and contrast' thesis statements

Remember, your thesis statement should clearly ❶show the topic, ❷the items you will describe about the topic, and ❸whether you are comparing, or contrasting, or comparing and contrasting.

Q: <u>Compare</u> drinking coffee at home to drinking coffee at a coffee shop.

> ❶Drinking coffee at home or at a coffee shop ❸is very similar. In either location a cup of coffee ❷can help a person to relax, and coffee drunk at home ❷tastes almost identical to coffee from a café.

Q: <u>Contrast</u> drinking coffee at home to drinking coffee at a coffee shop.

> ❶Although it may seem that drinking coffee at a café or at home is the same, ❸actually there are some big differences. Firstly, the ambience of a ❷café makes drinking coffee an experience rather than just an act of quenching thirst, and secondly, ❷coffee bought at a coffee shop is far more expensive.

Q: <u>Compare and contrast</u> drinking coffee at home to drinking coffee at a coffee shop.

> ❶Coffee drunk at home or at a coffee shop ❸can be both compared and contrasted. It is ❷alike in that coffee can help a person to relax irrespective of where it is drunk. ❷However, coffee bought at a coffee shop costs far more than coffee consumed at home.

Exercise 3c

Write thesis statements for the following questions. See the answer key at the back of the book to check your answers.

1 **Compare going jogging in the park to exercising at a gym.**

....

....

....

....

....

....

....

....

2 Contrast having fish as pets to having dogs as pets.

....

....

....

....

....

....

....

3 Compare and contrast watching sport to playing sport.

....

....

....

....

....

....

....

Skill B: Comparing and contrasting items from different perspectives

Look at this question and the two contrast passages underneath:

Q: Contrast pop music to classical music.

> **1** There are many differences between pop music and classical music. Two of the major disparities are that ❶pop music uses computers and technology to create songs whereas an orchestra plays classical music, and ❷pop music is usually faster and livelier than classical music.

> **2** There are many differences between pop music and classical music. Two of the major disparities are that ❶pop music uses computers and technology to create songs whereas an orchestra plays classical music, and ❷classical music is slower and more relaxing than pop music.

Notice how in the first passage both of the contrasts follow the format:
   ❶ pop > classical
   ❷ pop > classical

In the second passage the contrasts are written from different perspectives:
   ❶ pop > classical
   ❷ classical > pop

You can make your writing more interesting and varied by comparing and contrasting the items you will mention from different perspectives.

Exercise 3d

Using the given items, write a strong thesis statement for each of these questions making sure you use different perspectives.

1 Compare learning in a classroom to learning via the Internet.

Item 1	material prepared by teachers
Item 2	multimedia resources

....

....

....

....

2 Contrast living in university accommodation to living off-campus.

Item 1	more social
Item 2	less convenient

....

....

....

....

Further Practice

Write a <u>complete essay</u> for each of these questions. Once you have completed your essays, use this checklist to evaluate your writing.

Introduction	YES	NO
Does the introduction include a hook?		
Does the thesis statement state the topic, the items to be described about the topic, and is it clear whether the essay is a comparison, a contrast, or both?		
Body paragraphs	**YES**	**NO**
Is there an appropriate transition to begin the paragraph?		
Is there a clear topic sentence and is there a concluding sentence?		
Is there sufficient support for each advantage and each disadvantage?		
Is the structure correct for the type of question?		
Conclusion	**YES**	**NO**
Is there a clear conclusion transition?		
Does it state the topic and the items of difference?		

❶ Contrast working for a big company with running your own business.

Ideas box:

Contrast 1	
Contrast 2	

❷ **Compare and contrast the influence of celebrities on children to the influence of parents.**

Ideas box:

Comparison 1	
Comparison 2	
Contrast 1	
Contrast 2	

....

....

....

....

....

....

....

....

....

....

Section 2

Essay Types 2
Opinion | Preference | Agree/Disagree

Section 2

Essay Types 2

Unit 4 Writing Opinion Essays

Writing Focus

This type of question asks you to **give your opinion** on a topic, or it asks you to **defend an opinion** about a topic.

For instance, the following two questions are about the same topic. The first asks for your opinion:

> **Q:** Do you think that traveling abroad is essential for personal and professional development?

In this type of question <u>you can decide whether</u> you think traveling abroad is useful or not.

The question below is still about traveling abroad, but it provides a statement that you have to defend. This means you cannot choose the opposite view, but you must provide reasons why the statement is true (even if you don't agree!).

> **Q:** Traveling abroad is essential for personal and professional development. Give specific reasons supporting this viewpoint.

— **More to Know**

Common phrases in an 'opinion' question:

- Why is/are...?
- How can/could...?
- How is/does...?
- Do you...?
- What is the most important...?
- Why do you think...?
- What can be...?
- Has this...?
- Suggest...
- Give specific reasons supporting this viewpoint...
- Defend this statement with at least two reasons.
- Why is this?

How do I answer this type of question?

▶ The most important thing to answer this type of question is to provide at least two strong and logical reasons for your opinion that are credibly validated.

▶ It is your job to convince the reader that your opinion is correct. You must be consistent in your position, and you should concentrate on reinforcing and explaining your position as strongly as possible.

▶ Even though you are providing your opinion, it is preferable to write your answer in the third person (See STEP 1, Unit 9 – Academic Writing). Try to avoid phrases such as 'In my opinion.' The reader knows it is your opinion because you wrote it.

How do I structure an 'opinion/defend an opinion' essay?

- ▶ **Introduction**
- ▶ **Body paragraph 1** – first reason for your opinion
- ▶ **Body paragraph 2** – second reason for your opinion
- ▶ **Conclusion**

How do I write the introduction?

▶ The opening sentence for this type of essay should provide a hook and some background information on the topic. It often contains a paraphrase of the question.

▶ If you are asked to give your own opinion you must write a strong thesis statement that clearly tells the reader your opinion and the reasons for your opinion.

— More to Know

Useful words and phrases for 'opinion' introductions:

- The two main/major/primary reasons why ... is ... are
- ...for the following two reasons
- ... and ... are why ...
- The most important...
- ... can be ... in the following two ways. Firstly...

▶ If you are asked to defend an opinion, your thesis statement is usually a paraphrase of the question and the reasons that support the opinion.

— More to Know

Useful words and phrases for 'defend an opinion' introductions:

- Two reasons why ... is correct are ...
- (paraphrase of the question) because ... and ...

Let's *analyze* an introduction for this type of essay

Q: Suggest some reasons why people smoke and drink excessive amounts of alcohol.

(A) Why would anyone deliberately harm himself or herself? Despite knowing the health risks, many people drink a large amount of alcohol and smoke cigarettes. **(B)** Feeling the need to be part of a group and being unable to cope with stress are the main reasons why people smoke and drink even though they are permanently damaging their bodies.

A This is the opening sentence. It has a 'hook' to get the reader's attention, provides background information and general discussion of the topic, and paraphrases the question.

B This is the thesis statement. It provides two clear opinions on why the writer thinks people smoke and drink alcohol.

How do I write the body paragraphs?

▶ Write the first paragraph to explain in detail the first reason for your opinion. Make sure you do not add any information about your second reason. Write your second paragraph explaining your second reason.

▶ There must be a clear topic sentence for each paragraph. Each topic sentence must be 'expanded and explained.' There must be a clear concluding sentence for each paragraph too.

▶ It is very important that you validate and support your reasons convincingly. You must try to persuade the reader that your opinion is correct.

▶ You must use an appropriate transition between the two paragraphs. Both paragraphs are supporting the same viewpoint, so you should use transitions that 'introduce more points.'

— More to Know

Useful words and phrases for opinion body paragraphs:

Topic sentence phrases:
- **One of the explanations/motivations/rationales… is that…**
- **… is a significant factor…**
- **The** first/primary/main/major/most significant **reason…**

Transition words that introduce more points:

equally important	firstly (secondly, etc.)	furthermore	in addition
also	another	moreover	next
lastly	finally		

Transition words to introduce your examples and support:

for example	for instance	to illustrate	in fact
specifically	that is	as seen in	

Let's *analyze* a topic sentence, the validation and the support required for this type of essay

Q: Suggest some reasons why people smoke and drink excessive amounts of alcohol.

(A) Feeling the need to be part of a group is a significant factor in people smoking or drinking heavily. Most people wish to be liked and have lots of friends, and if a large proportion of a person's friends are smokers and/or drinkers that person can become excluded if he or she does not also smoke and/or drink. **(B)** For instance, a study in the US conducted by Carl Seltzer at Harvard University discovered that wishing to have status within a group is a substantial reason for people starting to smoke.
(C) It is clear that people smoke and drink in order to be part of a group.

(A) The topic sentence must state your opinion. You must then 'expand and explain' your opinion.

(B) Using a piece of research that can be checked by the reader adds strong support to your opinion. *See STEP 1, Unit 9 regarding correct citing of research.

(C) Make sure there is a concluding sentence that restates your opinion.

How do I write the conclusion?

▶ Use a clear 'conclusion transition.'
▶ The conclusion should re-state your opinion. It should also contain a final comment.
▶ It is very important to directly answer the question in your conclusion. You are trying to convince the reader that your opinions are correct, so you must make sure the reader is absolutely certain of your position as the last thing that they read.

— More to Know **Conclusion transitions:**

in conclusion	in summary	on the whole
therefore	to sum up	in short
for the reasons illustrated		

Let's *analyze* a conclusion for this type of essay:

Q: Suggest some reasons why people smoke and drink excessive amounts of alcohol.

A In short, **B** there must be very compelling reasons for people to deliberately harm themselves by knowingly smoking and drinking heavily. **C** This can only be explained by the basic human desire to be accepted into social environments, and by the need to find respite from the stress of modern day life.

A Use a 'conclusion transition' to begin the conclusion.

B In this conclusion the 'final comment' is stated before the summary of the writer's opinions. In this essay this is a good way of reinforcing the strength of the writer's opinions.

C Restate your opinions as creatively as possible.

Exercise 4a

1 Use the checklist to evaluate this introduction.

> I think Albert Einstein is the most influential person of the 20th century. His face is associated with the concept of genius.

Introduction	YES	NO
Is there an opening sentence that includes a 'hook'?		
Does the thesis statement clearly state the writer's opinion?		
Does the thesis statement give at least two valid reasons for the opinion?		
Is the opinion written in the third person?		

2 Use the checklist to evaluate this body paragraph.

> Firstly, Albert Einstein discovered the famous equation, $E=MC^2$. This was a major scientific breakthrough. He also wrote over 300 scientific papers and taught physics at one of the best universities in America. For example, he signed an important paper called the 'Russell-Einstein Manifesto' that highlighted the dangers of nuclear weapons.

Body paragraph	YES	NO
Is there a clear topic sentence and is there a concluding sentence?		
Does the writer 'expand and explain' the topic sentence?		
Is there sufficient support and is there sufficient validation for the opinion?		
Is there only one opinion given in the paragraph?		

3 Use the checklist to evaluate this conclusion.

> For the reasons illustrated, Albert Einstein is the greatest person of the 20th century. Albert Einstein completely altered the field of physics and his work enabled other scientists to discover things that have transformed our lives for the better. The world today would be a very different place had it not been for Albert Einstein.

Conclusion	YES	NO
Is there a clear conclusion transition?		
Does it restate the writer's opinions?		
Is there a final comment?		

Check your answers with the answer key at the back of the book.

Real Essays

In this section we will review an 'opinion' essay written by a Korean student of English.

step 1 — Read through the student's essay and highlight parts that could be improved. There is a note section at the end of the essay for you to write your ideas and comments.

Question: Do you think that traveling abroad is essential for personal and professional development?

In today globalized world, traveling abroad has become popular to a significant number of people. In Korea, many people travel to abroad for develop own ability. This rate is more and more increasing annually. Travel to abroad have a many advantages. Thus, this essay shows why travel abroad is good for personal and professional development.

Through the travel, we can get a many experiences. Travel is essential to improve our independence ability. For example, when people go to abroad, many people might be difficult to speak and read foreign languages. However, many people try to ask something to foreigner using body languages. Through this mistake, people able to meet many foreigners, and get a chance to talk to someone from a different nation and learn about it from him or her. In addition, we learned different countries culture too. Every country has an each nation's unique tradition location such as a tourist attraction. Through this tour, we get a wider personal point of view for professional development. If we travel in mother country, we already well knew our countries location and tourist attraction so travel time is just normal experiences to people. However, in travel abroad case, in particular students might feel that gave a chance that new environmental and exciting experience.

To sum up, traveling abroad is excellent choice for people who want to get a new experience and learn about different cultures. People can achieve adaptability which is necessary for develop in all aspects of their lives.

Your notes:

....

....

....

....

....

step 2 Here are some comments made by the marker of this essay. Compare the marker's comments with the items you found.

 Marker's Comments

Question: Do you think that traveling abroad is essential for personal and professional development?

In today's globalized world, traveling abroad has become popular to a significant number of people. In Korea, many people travel ~~to abroad for~~ to develop their own ability. This rate is increasing more and more ~~increasing~~ annually. Traveling to abroad ~~have a~~ has many advantages. Thus, this essay shows why travel abroad is good for personal and professional development.

- We 'go abroad,' 'go skiing,' 'go camping' etc. rather than 'go to abroad,' 'go to skiing,' 'go to camping.'

- These sentences need to be combined and expanded in order to make a coherent point. The rate might be increasing because traveling abroad has advantages.

- A stronger topic sentence is needed. You must state the reasons why traveling overseas is good for development.

Through ~~the~~ travel, ~~we~~ **people** ~~can get a~~ have many experiences. Travel is essential to improve ~~our~~ independence ~~ability~~. For example, when people go ~~to~~ abroad, many people might ~~be~~ have difficultly ~~to~~ speaking and reading foreign languages. However, many people try to ask something to foreigners using body languages. **Through this mistake**, people are able to meet many foreigners, and get a chance to talk to someone from a different nation and learn about **it** from him or her. In addition, ~~we~~ people can ~~learned~~ about a different country's~~ies~~ culture too. Every country has ~~an each nation's~~ unique and traditional locations, such as a **tourist attraction**. Through this **tour**, ~~we~~ people get a wider **personal point of view for professional development**. If ~~we~~ people travel in their mother country, ~~we~~ they already know well ~~knew our~~ the country's~~ies~~ location and tourist attractions, so travel ~~time~~ is just a normal experiences ~~to people~~. However, in the case of traveling abroad ~~case~~, in particular students might feel that it **gave** a chance ~~that~~ for new **environmental** and exciting experiences.

To sum up, traveling abroad is an excellent choice for people who want to **get** a new experience and learn about different cultures. People can achieve the adaptability which is necessary for development in all aspects of their lives.

- Use the third person.
- What 'mistake'? Although the point is valid (perhaps you can become more independent by having to use another language), it is not really used explicitly enough to validate your opinion. "Having to make yourself understood in a foreign environment forces a person to be more independent. For example..."
- To what does 'it' refer?
- This point is a bit weak and is not supported. Exactly how does sightseeing help a person develop personally and professionally?
- This might not be the best word choice. You are referring to the act of traveling abroad in order to develop, whereas the word 'tour' is more for commonly associated with a leisure vacation.
- This needs to be expanded and explained. How does having a wider personal point of view develop somebody professionally?
- Be consistent with your tense.
- The word 'environmental' is a bit random and unexpected. How is it related to personal and professional development?
- 'have a new experience' is more common.

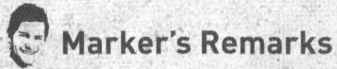 **Marker's Remarks**

Your use of English is quite good, although you must be consistent in tone and tense. The introduction starts well, but your thesis statement needs to include the reasons for your opinion.

The content of your answer needs a little more definition. Your first point is about learning independence. This should be explicitly stated in the first paragraph's topic sentence, and then you can use your example as validation. Your second point (learning another culture) needs to be in separate paragraph.

Perhaps a better structure would be to use one paragraph to show how travel can help a person develop personally, and a second paragraph to show how a person can develop professionally.

step 3 Here is the same question answered by a native-English speaker:

The world these days is a small place. Journeys that used to take weeks can now be done in hours, and experiences that were out of reach are now easily obtained. However, I do not think that traveling abroad is essential for personal and professional development.

Personal development can be achieved in a variety of ways. It could be argued that travel could help a person enhance their personal skills, but travel is not absolutely necessary. People have access to all types of media including the Internet, worldwide TV and the radio, and information is easily available about all the different views, opinions and cultures of the world. For example, by watching global news programmes people can learn to think about things in a more open-minded and considerate manner.
We can all learn vicariously through the media and gain the skills and knowledge we need to advance our personal lives.

Likewise, going to a foreign country is not compulsory to improve professionally. In reality, only a very small proportion of the workforce actually travels overseas or deals with people from other countries. For instance, an accountant for a small company would improve his or her career prospects far more by obtaining further qualifications than he or she would by spending some time abroad.
For most people who are fortunate to live in the developed world there are plenty of opportunities to expand their professional capabilities in their own country.

So, this essay has demonstrated that traveling abroad is not required for personal and professional development. People should stay at home and save their money instead.

Exercise 4b

Examine the essay written by the <u>native speaker of English</u> and answer the following questions. See the answer key at the back of the book for explanations.

1 What synonyms and/or alternative phrases were used for the following words:

development:
....

essential:
....

abroad:
....

2 The introduction and conclusion are weak in the essay. List some of the reasons why they are not very good.

Introduction:
....

....

Conclusion:
....

....

3 Use this checklist to evaluate both body paragraphs of the essay.

	YES	NO
Is there a clear topic sentence in each paragraph?		
Is there a clear concluding sentence in each paragraph?		
Are there clear transitions to begin each paragraph?		
Does each paragraph contain one opinion that is adequately expanded and explained?		
Is each opinion adequately validated?		
Is each opinion directly relevant to answering the question?		

Essential Skills

Skill A: Writing clear and precise opinions

▶ Your opinion must be clearly stated. If the reader is not sure of your position you have not stated it clearly enough.

▶ Your opinion must be precise, which means it must be specific rather than general: "Going to music concert is more entertaining and rewarding than listening to a CD" is better than "Live music is better than recorded music."

▶ You must make sure your opinion is directly relevant and answers the question.

Let's *look at* some examples:

Q: Do children learn more by watching television or by learning to play a musical instrument?

Children learn in all types of different ways, including by watching television. Also, learning to play a musical instrument is very beneficial too.	It is not absolutely clear whether the writer thinks learning to play an instrument is the way children learn more. It would be better as: "While children can learn from the TV, they learn far more by learning to play a musical instrument."
Music is so beautiful and calming. Without music life can be very dull and boring so learning to play an instrument is one of the best things to do.	This tells us that the writer likes music and thinks it is a good idea to learn an instrument, but it does not answer the question – we do not know whether the writer thinks children learn more from learning to play music rather than watching TV.

Exercise 4c

1 The following passage does not give a clear and precise opinion. Rewrite the passage to make the writer's opinion clearer.

> Q: What can governments do to make people save for their retirement?
>
> **Making sure people save for their future is a challenge for the government. The government needs to find a solution to this problem using things like tax, especially considering that most developed countries have an ageing population.**

2 **The following passage is not directly relevant to the question. Rewrite the passage to directly answer the question.**

> Q: Why do you think people watch movies?
>
> **There are so many types of movies, such as thrillers, horror movies, comedies, and romantic films, that it is easy for anybody to find the type of film that interests them.**

....

....

....

....

....

....

....

....

Example answers are in the answer key at the back of the book.

Skill B: Validating your opinions

▶ People might disagree with your opinion, so you must validate your viewpoint as robustly as possible.

Let's *look at* an example of validating an opinion:

Learning to play a musical instrument is far better for a child than watching television. By learning music, a child naturally develops skills that cannot easily be obtained just by watching TV. **For instance, a study in the US conducted on 7-year olds by Professor Shaw of the University of California concluded that children actually learn math skills while playing instruments. "When children learn rhythm, they are learning ratios, fractions and proportions," he said.**

> This is the validation. Some people might disagree with your opinion, but it is hard to disagree with relevant and valid scientific research.

▶ The main ways to validate your opinion were covered in STEP 1, Unit 4:

- **Personal experience.** This is the easiest type of validation to use if you are writing your essay for an exam such as TOEFL or IELTS. However, a personal experience does not provide as strong validation as something like scientific research.
- **Scientific research.** Citing a real and valid piece of research often provides the strongest validation for an opinion. See STEP 1, Unit 9 about how to cite correctly.
- **A quotation.** This can be the hardest way to validate an opinion, and should only be used if you are absolutely sure that the quotation is completely and directly relevant to your opinion.
- **A well-known fact or statement.** This is a good way to provide stronger validation if you are writing in exam conditions. It provides a bit more support to your opinion than a personal experience.

Exercise 4d

Read this beginning to a paragraph. It contains a topic sentence and has been expanded a little. Write some validation for this paragraph according to the instructions in the question:

> **Learning to play a musical instrument is far better for a child than watching television. By learning music, a child naturally develops skills that cannot easily be obtained just by watching TV.**

❶ Validate it using a personal experience.

....

....

....

....

....

❷ Validate it using a well-known fact about music.

....

....

....

....

....

❸ Validate it using one of these quotations about music from the box.

> - **Music is the medicine of the mind. -John A. Logan**
>
> - **Music expresses feeling and thought, without language; it was below and before speech, and it is above and beyond all words. -Robert G. Ingersoll**
>
> - **Music produces a kind of pleasure which human nature cannot do without. -Confucius**

....

....

....

....

Think about which method was easiest to use to validate the opinion. Which method provides the strongest validation?
Example answers are in the answers section at the back of the book.

Further Practice

Write a <u>complete essay</u> for each of these questions. Once you have completed your essays, use this checklist to evaluate your writing.

Introduction	YES	NO
Is there an opening sentence that includes a 'hook'?		
Does the thesis statement clearly indicate my opinion and the reasons for my opinion?		
Is the question paraphrased somewhere in the introduction?		
Body paragraphs	**YES**	**NO**
Are there clear topic and concluding sentences?		
Is there only one opinion in each paragraph?		
Is each opinion clear and precise?		
Is each opinion expanded and explained?		
Is each opinion directly relevant to the question?		
Is there sufficient validation for each opinion?		
Is there a clear contrast transition between the two paragraphs?		
Conclusion	**YES**	**NO**
Have I included a clear conclusion transition?		
Have I restated my opinion forcefully?		
Have I directly answered the question in the conclusion?		

1 **Why is watching or reading the news important?**

Ideas box:

Opinion 1	
Opinion 2	

2 People are often nicer to their friends than they are to their family. Why is this?

Ideas box:

Opinion 1	
Opinion 2	

....

....

....

....

....

....

....

....

....

....

....

Unit 5 Writing Preference Essays

Writing Focus

This type of question usually gives you two statements or opinions and then asks which one you **prefer** or which one you **agree with**.

> *e.g.* Some people prefer to live in a small town. Others prefer to live in a big city. Which place would you prefer to live in?
>
> Some people believe that a college or university education should be available to all students. Others believe that higher education should be available only to good students. Which view do you agree with?

— More to Know

Common phrases in a 'preference' question:

- Which do you prefer?
- Which of these do you recommend?
- Which do you think is better?
- Which would you choose?
- Which view do you agree with?

How do I answer this type of question?
▶ It is a good idea to 'acknowledge' the statement or opinion you do not prefer.

▶ You must answer the question by clearly and directly stating in the introduction which of the two points you prefer or agree with. However, it is better to write in the third person rather than the first person (see STEP 1, Unit 9 – Academic Writing) except if you give a personal example as validation for your point within the body paragraphs.

▶ You must give at least two reasons why you prefer or agree with one of the statements or opinions.

How do I structure a 'preference' essay?
▶ **Introduction** – acknowledge the statement/opinion which you do not prefer and then state your position in a strong thesis statement.
▶ **Body paragraph 1** – The main reason for your preference.
▶ **Body paragraph 2** – The second reason for your preference.
▶ **Conclusion** – acknowledge the other statement/opinion again, and briefly summarize the reasons for your preference.

How do I write the introduction?
▶ You do not need to write a 'hook' for this type of answer. Instead, simply paraphrase the two statements/opinions in your first sentence.

▶ Then, 'acknowledge' the statement/opinion that you do not prefer or agree with. Start this sentence with one of the words that acknowledges a different viewpoint from your own:

To acknowledge the other viewpoint before stating your viewpoint:			
whereas	granted that	even though	though
while	although		

▶ Finish this sentence with your thesis statement. The thesis statement must state the exact reasons for your preference.

— **More to Know**

Useful words and phrases for 'preference' introductions:

- **Whereas (opposing statement/opinion)**, it is more desirable (your preference) because…
- **Although (opposing statement/opinion)** it is preferable (your preference) due to…
- **Even though (opposing statement/opinion)** , (your preference) is far better for the following two reasons . Firstly…

Let's *analyze* an introduction for this type of essay

Q: Some people prefer to spend most of their time alone. Others like to be with friends most of the time. Do you prefer to spend your time alone or with friends?

(A) How people spend their time is a matter of preference. Some people like to be with friends most of the time while others prefer to be alone. (B) Whereas being by oneself can be nice at times, (C) it is better to be with friends most of the time for the following two reasons. Firstly, being with friends helps a person to relax. Secondly, a person can receive information and advice from their friends that they might not discover if they spend too much time alone.

A This is a simple paraphrase of the question.

B This acknowledges the other viewpoint and uses an appropriate transition.

C This is the thesis statement.

How do I write the body paragraphs?

▶ Write the first paragraph to explain the main reason for your preference, and write the second paragraph to explain the second reason.

▶ There must be a clear topic sentence and concluding sentence for each paragraph.

▶ Each reason for your preference must be explained and supported by appropriate reasons and logic.

▶ Relevant and appropriate examples should be included. While the majority of your essay should be written in the third person, it is acceptable to write a personal experience in the first person.

▶ You must use an appropriate transition between the two paragraphs. Use an 'addition transition' to begin the second paragraph because you are adding another reason.

— More to Know

Useful words and phrases for 'preference' body paragraphs:

<u>Topic sentence phrases:</u>
- It is very important…
- … is preferable/desirable/superior because…
- Firstly/secondly, people can/must /are able to /should…

<u>'Addition transition' words to introduce the second paragraph:</u>

equally important	secondly	furthermore	in addition
also	another	moreover	next
lastly	finally		

Let's *analyze* a topic sentence for this type of essay

Q: Some people prefer to spend most of their time alone. Others like to be with friends most of the time. Do you prefer to spend your time alone or with friends?

^AFurthermore, ^Bpeople are able to gain knowledge, advice and information from their friends.

A Use an 'addition transition' to begin the second paragraph.

B The topic sentence must clearly state the reason for your preference.

How do I write the conclusion?
▶ Use a clear 'conclusion transition.'

▶ The conclusion should again acknowledge the statement/opinion you do not prefer, and must briefly summarize your preference and reasons.

Conclusion transitions:

in conclusion	in summary	on the whole	therefore
to sum up	in short	for the reasons illustrated	

129

Let's *analyze* a conclusion for this type of essay:

Q: Some people prefer to spend most of their time alone. Others like to be with friends most of the time. Do you prefer to spend your time alone or with friends?

(A) For the reasons illustrated, **(B)** spending a good proportion of time with friends is preferable to spending too much time alone. **(C)** Friends can help a person to relax, and they are a source of valuable information and advice.

(A) Use a 'conclusion transition' to begin the conclusion.

(B) This part of the sentence restates your preference and acknowledges the other statement/opinion.

(C) This sentence briefly restates the reasons for your preference.

Exercise 5a

The following paragraphs were written in response to this question:

> **Q:** Some people think that children should begin their formal education at a very early age and should spend most of their time on school studies. Others believe that young children should spend most of their time playing. Which view do you agree with?

❶ Use the checklist to evaluate this introduction.

> **It is vital that children go to school and study formerly at an early age. If they start their education too late they can fall behind their peers academically. In addition, young children make friends at school so it is important for them socially as well as academically.**

Introduction	YES	NO
Does the introduction paraphrase the question?		
Is the other statement/opinion acknowledged?		
Is there an appropriate transition to introduce the other statement/opinion?		
Is there a strong thesis statement?		

2 **Use the checklist to evaluate this body paragraph.**

> **Furthermore, my friend started school much later than most other people in my class and he still sometimes feels a little bit isolated. In a recent sports class he was the last person to be chosen for a team and this experience made him feel sad.**

Body paragraph	YES	NO
Is there an appropriate transition to begin the paragraph?		
Is there a clear topic sentence and is there a concluding sentence?		
Is there sufficient explanation for the preference?		
Is there an example to reinforce the preference?		

3 **Use the checklist to evaluate this conclusion.**

> **In summary, it is advisable that children begin their formal education at a young age. While there are some benefits of playing, it is important that a child is on the same academic level and has the same social exposure as his or her peers.**

Conclusion	YES	NO
Is there a clear conclusion transition?		
Does it clearly restate the preference?		
Does it acknowledge the other statement/opinion?		
Does it briefly summarize the reasons for the preference?		

Check your answer with the answer key at the back of the book.

Real Essays

In this section we will review a 'preference' essay written by a Korean student of English.

step 1 Read through the student's essay and highlight parts that could be improved. There is a note section at the end of the essay for you to write your ideas and comments.

Question: Some students prefer to study alone. Others prefer to study with a group of students. Which do you prefer? Use specific reasons and examples to support your answer.

In these days, study group is the main trend amongst students who try to study efficiently. Also parents are interested in these study group workings because of their kids. More and more study groups are specialized in some parts and becoming bigger and bigger. However, can we get better result than studying alone? No, it is not. The result of what we have studied is more magnified when we study alone than studying through groups.

There are several reasons why we should study alone. I will tell you the main three reasons. First, we can concentrate in our studies. I think, when lots of people, maybe just 2 or 3 people, they do not concentrate on their studies, they usually do other things which disturb their study. Chatting can be the most typical interruption when we are doing group studying. But studying alone does not make any noises.

Second, we can get more time. Frankly speaking, group study is a huge time consuming. We have to make a plan to study like where shall we meet, when, and also who are the members to study with. This process takes lots of time from us. Not just this process, but also other things which takes time in preparing the group study.

For these two reasons, we can get a better results by studying alone. In the case, if you really want to do group studying, I will give you a tip which you can enjoy both things. The answer is "reading room." In this place, you can study in groups, and also study alone.

Your notes:

....

....

....

....

....

 Here are some comments made by the marker of this essay. Compare the marker's comments with the items you found.

Question: Some students prefer to study alone. Others prefer to study with a group of students. Which do you prefer? Use specific reasons and examples to support your answer.

In tThese days, a study group is the main trend amongst students who try to study efficiently. Also parents are interested in these study group workings because of their kids children. More and more study groups are specialized in some parts subjects and are becoming bigger and bigger. However, can we get better results than studying alone? No, it is we cannot. The result of what we have studied is more magnified when we study alone than when we studying through in groups.

 Marker's Comments

- This is not completely relevant to the question. The question is asking whether you prefer to study alone or in a group.

- This is too informal.

- Be careful using questions in your answers. A question can be used for effect, but often it just seems unnatural.

- If you do use a question make sure it is answered directly. "Can we..." must be answered, "No, we cannot."

- Not quite the best word choice or sentence composition here. "We retain far more of what we study when we are alone than when we are in a group."

134

There are several reasons why we should study alone. I will tell you the main two reasons. First, we can concentrate in on our studies. I think, when there are lots of people, maybe just 2 or 3 people, they do not concentrate on their studies, they usually do other things which that disturb their study. Chatting can be the most typical interruption when we are doing group studying. But studying alone does not make any noises.

Second, we can get more time. Frankly speaking, group study is a hugely time consuming. We have to make a plan to study; like where shall we meet, when, and also who are the members to study with. This process takes lots of time from us. Not just this process, but also other things which takes time in preparing the group study.

For these two reasons, we can get a better results by studying alone. In the case, if that you really want to do group studying, I will give you a tip which you can enjoy both things. The answer is a "reading room." In this place, you can study in groups, and also study alone.

- This should be part of your thesis statement – not part of your first body paragraph. Also, try to avoid writing in the first person unless you are giving a personal experience as an example, and avoid informal phrases such as 'I will tell you.' "There are several reasons why we should study alone: X and Y."

- '2 or 3' is probably not 'lots.' If you are trying to say that just 2 or 3 people will disturb concentration it would be better to write: "When there is a group, even a small group of just two or three people, people find it harder to concentrate on their studies." Spell small numbers in academic writing – 'two' not 2.

- In this paragraph you have used 'I,' 'we' and 'they.' Try to be consistent and write in the third person.

- You need to expand this sentence to make a complete statement. "Second, a person will have more actual learning time if they study alone."

- This is too informal. It would be better to write 'In fact' or 'Actually' to introduce this type of statement.

- You need to mention what these 'other things' actually are, and then you must explain the relevance they have to not studying as effectively as if you were alone.

- This is too informal.

- This point is not really relevant to answering the question. Your conclusion should restate why your preference is to study alone.

 **Marker's Remarks**

Overall, you have done a good job of expressing your preference – the reader is in no doubt that you would prefer to study alone.

The introduction is perhaps a little too long if you are answering a TOEFL or IELTS essay; there is a little bit of redundant information.
Also be very careful with the structure of your introduction – actually part of your thesis statement is written in the first body paragraph.

In your body paragraphs make sure that each paragraph has a clear topic sentence and a clear concluding sentence. Both paragraphs lack a concluding sentence that finalizes your point. Some examples could validate your points more strongly.

Try to write in the third person for exam questions and academic writing – the reader knows it is your opinion because you wrote it. However, it is acceptable to write in the first person if you are giving a personal experience as an example in your body paragraph.

The first sentence in your conclusion is strong and direct, but then the next part is not really relevant.

step 3 Here is the same question answered by a native-English speaker:

People like to study in different ways; some prefer to be by themselves and others like to study in a group. While studying alone can sometimes be beneficial, it is better to study in a group. Studying with other people not only motivates a person to learn, it also offers opportunities to obtain new perspectives and understanding that a person could not grasp if alone.

A person can use the knowledge and abilities of the other students to improve their own skills. There are very few students who know everything, or who can grasp every single concept by themselves. By being part of a group and discussing difficult topics, a person can gain insights and knowledge that they could not get if they studied in solitude. This point can be illustrated by the well-known phrase 'two heads are better than one.' Therefore, group studying will help a person to understand ideas more easily and lead to an improved learning outcome.

Furthermore, motivation is one of the most important aspects of successful study and a study group can increase a person's enthusiasm to study in many ways. Not only does being part of a group make a person feel obliged to attend the study session so that they do not disappoint the other members, once a person is in the group he or she will feel a certain amount of competition with the other members. For example, my brother was a lazy student until he joined a study group. He told me that he felt obliged to attend each meeting and hated to score the lowest grade in the group. So by being part of a group a person is not only encouraged to start learning because they must attend each session, they will study harder to ensure they do not fall behind their peers.

In conclusion, studying in a group is preferable to cramming alone. Whereas it can be hard to find the incentive to study by oneself, it is easy to be motivated as part of a group. Likewise, ideas can be hard to grasp by oneself but in a group a person has the chance to receive help from the other participants.

Exercise 5b

Examine the essay written by the native speaker of English and answer the following questions. See the answer key at the back of the book for explanations.

1 What synonyms and/or alternative phrases were used for the following words:

alone:
....

motivation:
....

study:
....

members:
....

2 List the transition words and transition phrases used in the essay.

....

....

....

3 Use this checklist to evaluate both body paragraphs of the essay.

	YES	NO
Is there a clear topic sentence in each paragraph?		
Is there a clear concluding sentence in each paragraph?		
Is there sufficient 'expansion and explanation' of the topic sentence?		
Is the order in which the points are made the same as in the 'thesis statement'?		
Is each point adequately validated?		
Is there a clear transition between the two paragraphs?		

Essential Skills

Skill A: Acknowledging the other statement or opinion

Being able to use correctly formed sentences that acknowledge an opposing view before stating your viewpoint is an important skill for this type of essay that will improve your writing.

The words that can be used for this skill are:

> **To acknowledge the other viewpoint before stating your viewpoint:**
>
> whereas   granted that   even though   though
> while   although
>
> **Preference phrases:**
> it is more desirable   it is preferable
> it is far better   it is advisable

Let's *look at* an example:

> ❶Acknowledgement > ❷opposing view > ❸preference phrase > ❹your view > because > ❺reasons
>
> ❶Even though ❷eating pizza is delicious, ❸it is far better to ❹eat an apple because ❺an apple is healthier and less expensive.

Exercise 5c

Use the 'acknowledgement' words and 'preference phrases' to create correct sentences that acknowledge the other viewpoint. Use the boxes to note your points.

1 Do you prefer to take a vacation abroad or in your own country?

Opposing view	
Your view	
Reason 1	
Reason 2	

Your points:

....

....

....

....

2 **Would you prefer to live in an apartment or in a house?**

Opposing view	
Your view	
Reason 1	
Reason 2	

Your points:
....

....

....

....

3 **Do you prefer eating home-cooked food or restaurant food?**

Opposing view	
Your view	
Reason 1	
Reason 2	

Your points:
....

....

....

....

Skill B: Expressing your preference using the third person or impersonally

Writing in the third person is preferable to writing in the first person, except when you are giving a personal example as the 'validation' part of a body paragraph. (See STEP 1, Unit 9 – Academic Writing for more on this topic)

Let's *look at* how to change first person writing to third person writing:

First person:
Although **I think that** living in a big city has some advantages, **I would prefer** to live in the countryside because the air is cleaner and people are friendlier.

Third person/impersonally:
Although living in a big city has some advantages, **it is preferable** to live in the countryside because the air is cleaner and people are friendlier.

Exercise 5d

Rewrite the following sentences in the third person or impersonally. Try to make the sentence more formal and/or more complete if necessary. Sample answers are in the answer key at the back of the book.

1 While I love to read novels sometimes, I actually prefer to read non-fiction as I can learn more real facts and I think non-fiction is better written.

....

....

....

2 Though I like the idea of moving to another town, it is better for me to stay in my hometown because my friends are here and I know where everything is.

....

....

....

3 I prefer to get up early. I don't like to get up late.

....

....

....

Further Practice

Write a complete essay for each of these questions. Once you have completed your essays, use this checklist to evaluate your writing.

Introduction	YES	NO
Does the introduction paraphrase the question?		
Is the other statement/opinion acknowledged?		
Is there an appropriate transition to introduce the other statement/opinion?		
Is there a strong thesis statement?		
Body paragraphs	YES	NO
Is there a clear topic sentence in each paragraph?		
Is there a clear concluding sentence in each paragraph?		
Is there sufficient 'expansion and explanation' of the topic sentence?		
Is the order in which the points are made the same as in the 'thesis statement'?		
Is each point adequately validated?		
Is there a clear transition between the two paragraphs?		
Conclusion	YES	NO
Is there a clear conclusion transition?		
Does it clearly restate the preference?		
Does it acknowledge the other statement/opinion?		
Does it briefly summarize the reasons for the preference?		

❶ **Some people like to plan a detailed itinerary for their vacation. Other people do not plan their vacation in detail. Which do you prefer? Give specific reasons for your preference.**

Ideas box:

Preference	
Reason 1	
Reason 2	

2 Some people believe that people who smoke should pay more for medical treatment. Other people believe that the cost of medical treatment should be the same for smokers and non-smokers. Which opinion do you agree with? Use specific reasons and detail to support your answer.

Ideas box:

Preference	
Reason 1	
Reason 2	

Unit 6 Writing Agree/Disagree Essays

Writing Focus

This type of question asks **whether you agree or disagree with a statement or viewpoint**. The question will always contain the words 'agree or disagree,' but sometimes they will be at the beginning of the question, and sometimes at the end. For example:

> Q: Do you agree or disagree with the following statement? Playing games teaches us about life.
>
> Q: Playing games teaches us about life. Do you agree or disagree?

— More to Know

Common phrases in an 'agree or disagree' question:

- Do you agree or disagree...?

How do I answer this type of question?

▶ You must answer the question by clearly and directly stating whether you agree or disagree in the introduction. However, it is better to write in the third person rather than the first person (see STEP 1, Unit 9 – Academic Writing).

▶ You will need to give at least two detailed reasons why you agree or why you disagree.

How do I structure an 'agree/disagree' essay?

- An **Introduction** that clearly indicates whether you agree or disagree and has a hook that gets the reader's attention.
- **Body paragraph 1** – the main reason you agree (or disagree)
- **Body paragraph 2** – the second reason you agree (or disagree)
- **Conclusion**

How do I write the introduction?

- First, write a 'hook' that engages the reader.

- Then, in your thesis statement indicate whether you agree or disagree with the question statement, and give your two reasons. It is better not to use the words 'agree' or 'disagree'!

- Most of the time you will need to use the question statement in your thesis statement. Sometimes you can paraphrase the question statement, but this is not always necessary.

— More to Know

Useful words and phrases for agree/disagree introductions:

<u>These can be used whether you agree or disagree:</u>
- It is true/not true that (question statement). Firstly,...
- The statement that (question statement) is correct / incorrect because... and...

<u>These can be used if you disagree:</u>
- Although some people believe that (question statement), this statement is not accurate as... and...
- While it could be argued that (question statement), it is not true because... and...

<u>These can be used if you agree:</u>
- Even though (opposite sentiment of question statement), the statement that (question statement) is true. Firstly,...
- The statement that (question statement) is correct. Although some people may contend that (opposite sentiment of question statement) their opinions are not correct for the following reasons. Firstly,...

Let's *analyze* some introductions for this type of essay

▶ **Disagree** with the question statement:

Q: Do you agree or disagree with the following statement? ᴬSometimes it is better not to tell the truth.

ᴮWould you be happy with yourself if you told a big lie to your best friend?
ᶜSome people believe that ⁽¹⁾sometimes it is better not to tell the truth, ⁽²⁾but this is a misguided view. Firstly, being truthful and honest at all times is a fundamental component of being a decent human being. Secondly, when people lie there are often unforeseen and tragic consequences.

Ⓐ This is the question statement.

Ⓑ This is the hook. It asks the reader a question to consider.

Ⓒ In this type of essay you can write your thesis statement directly after the hook. Notice ⁽¹⁾that the writer has directly copied the question statement and ⁽²⁾how the writer has given his or her position (disagree) without using the actual word 'disagree.'

▶ **Agree** with the question statement:

Q: Do you agree or disagree with the following statement? ᴬSometimes it is better not to tell the truth.

ᴮAccording to Oscar Wilde, "The truth is rarely pure and never simple".
ᶜEven though ⁽¹⁾telling the truth as much as possible is something that everybody should strive to achieve, ⁽²⁾the statement that sometimes it is better not to tell the truth is correct. Firstly, sometimes people need to be protected from the truth, and sometimes a small lie can make people happier than if they were told the truth.

Ⓐ This is the question statement.

Ⓑ This is the hook. It uses a quotation from a famous author.

Ⓒ In this type of essay you can write your thesis statement directly after the hook. Notice ⁽¹⁾how the writer has used his or her own words to show the opposite meaning of the question statement and ⁽²⁾that the writer has directly copied the question statement.

How do I write the body paragraphs?

▶ The structure of the body part of your essay for this type of question is very similar to writing a preference essay.

▶ Write the first paragraph to explain the main reason why you agree or why you disagree, and write the second paragraph to explain the second reason.

▶ There must be a clear topic sentence and concluding sentence for each paragraph.

▶ Each reason why you agree (or disagree) must be explained and supported by appropriate reasons and logic.

▶ Relevant and appropriate examples should be included. While the majority of your essay should be written in the third person, it is acceptable to write a personal experience in the first person.

▶ You must use an appropriate transition between the two paragraphs. Use an 'addition transition' to begin the second paragraph because you are adding another reason.

— More to Know

Useful words and phrases for 'agree or disagree' body paragraphs:

Topic sentence phrases:
- The first/second reason why the statement is correct/incorrect is…
- The main/primary/most important reason that the statement is true/not true is that…
- One of the main reasons / another reason why (question statement) is valid/invalid is…

'Addition transition' words to introduce the second paragraph:

equally important	secondly	furthermore	in addition
also	another	moreover	next
lastly	finally		

Let's *analyze* a topic sentence for this type of essay

Q: Do you agree or disagree with the following statement? Sometimes it is better not to tell the truth.

The most important reason why people should always tell the truth is that honesty and integrity are two of the most important traits of being a good person.

> The topic sentence must clearly state one of the reasons mentioned in your thesis statement.

How do I write the conclusion?

▶ Use a clear 'conclusion transition.'

▶ The conclusion should paraphrase your thesis statement and provide a final comment in answer to your hook.

— More to Know

Useful words and phrases for 'agree or disagree' conclusions:

Conclusion transitions:

in conclusion	in summary	on the whole	therefore
to sum up	in short	for the reasons illustrated	

Let's *analyze* a conclusion for this type of essay:

Q: Do you agree or disagree with the following statement? Sometimes it is better not to tell the truth.

A For the reasons illustrated, **B** it is occasionally necessary to withhold the truth so that people are not unnecessarily hurt or exposed to harmful occurrences.
C As Oscar Wilde intimated in his famous quote, the truth is often complicated and rarely innocent.

A Use a 'conclusion transition' to begin the conclusion.

B For this type of essay you just need to paraphrase your thesis statement.

C A final comment to reinforce the validity of the argument

Exercise 6a

1 Use the checklist to evaluate this introduction.

> I like money, but I like my friends more. Therefore I agree with the statement that borrowing money from friends can lead to harm. My brother lent $50 to one of his friends but he never got the money back. They ended up having a fight so you definitely should not borrow money from friends.

Introduction	YES	NO
Is there an opening sentence that includes a 'hook'?		
Is there a strong thesis statement that includes the question statement and explicit reasons?		
Is the introduction written in the third person?		

2 Use the checklist to evaluate this body paragraph.

> In the first instance, it is often very difficult to ask a friend to return the money. Sometimes even friends have different opinions on when the money should be returned. I once borrowed a few dollars from my best friend and thought I could give the money back to him a week later, but he wanted the money the next day. I didn't have the money, so we argued. This example clearly shows that it is hard to ask for the money back sometimes.

Body paragraph	YES	NO
Is there a clear topic sentence and is there a concluding sentence?		
Is there sufficient expansion of the topic sentence?		
Is there sufficient and appropriate validation of the reason?		

3 Use the checklist to evaluate this conclusion.

> **Therefore, borrowing money from friends can lead to harm. It can lead to arguments and it can make one friend feel inferior to the other. I like money, but I like my friends better.**

Conclusion	YES	NO
Is there a clear conclusion transition?		
Does it paraphrase the essay statement, including specific reasons?		
Does it answer the hook?		

Real Essays

In this section we will review an 'agree/disagree' essay written by a Korean student of English.

  Read through the student's essay and highlight parts that could be improved. There is a note section at the end of the essay for you to write your ideas and comments.

Question: Do you agree or disagree with the following statement? Reading a book a second time is more interesting than reading it the first time. Use reasons and examples to support your answer.

I have read the book 'The Little Prince' for several times. I first read it when I was around seven. For me at that time, 'The Little Prince' meant nothing than a boring story. And I read it for the second time when I was about ten. Then I saw the different characteristics of people living in each star, and found out the layout of the story. And in the third time of reading that before, around three days before, I found out the author's vision about world and the true meaning of love. Not only have the book 'The Little Prince,' but also many other books seemed different in every time one read the book. Therefore it is more interesting to read a book for a second time than reading it the first time.

First, one can found hidden information on the book in the second time. It is hard to catch all information from a non-fiction book in the first time. But when it is read again and again, one can find out what is important and what is not, and some hidden information. It is the same way that one can get a better score than people who read the textbook just once when he or she read it twice or more.

In addition, reading the book for the second time is more interesting because the sentiment of that day depends the feeling after reading the book. Even reading the same book, the feeling can be vary when reading it in a gloomy day or in a very exciting day. We can see different parts of each book.

> To sum up, I think the second time of reading the book would be more entertaining than the first time because we can look at the book in the different vision. Finding another face of the book is the most enjoyable part in reading the book. In this way, reading in the second time is the 'real' reading.

Your notes:
....
....
....
....
....
....
....
....
....
....
....
....
....

step 2 Here are some comments made by the marker of this essay. Compare the marker's comments with the items you found.

 Marker's Comments

Question: Do you agree or disagree with the following statement? Reading a book a second time is more interesting than reading it the first time. Use reasons and examples to support your answer.

I have read the book 'The Little Prince' for several times. I first read it when I was around seven years old. For me At that time, 'The Little Prince' meant nothing other than a boring story. And I read it for the second time when I was about ten. Then I saw the different characteristics of people living in each star, and found out the layout of the story. And in at the third time of reading that before, around three days before, I found out the author's vision about the world and the true meaning of love. Not only have the book 'The Little Prince,' but also many other books seemed different in every time one reads the book. Therefore it is more interesting to read a book for a second time than reading it the first time.

First, one can found find hidden information on the a book in the second time. It is hard to catch all information from a non-fiction book in the first time. But when it is read again and again, one can find out what is important and what is not, and one can also find some hidden information. It is the same way that one can get a better score than people who read the a textbook just once when he or she read it twice or more.

- It is hard to write this particular sentence in the third person, but always remember that it is preferable to write in the third person if possible.

- Try to avoid beginning sentences with conjunctions.

- Unless the reader knows the story of 'The Little Prince,' this does not make sense. "...people in the book."

- Is 'layout' the best word choice here? What exactly do you mean – the structure of the story or the meaning of the story?

- I am not sure what this means.

- Overall, a good introduction although it might be a bit long compared to the rest of your essay. You have provided a lot of background information (your experience of 'The Little Prince), and a thesis statement. However, you should include the actual reasons in the thesis statement.

- You are not now referring to a specific book so you should use 'a.'

- Better as "...in the second time of reading."

- The analogy is excellent, but the construction needs to be improved a little. "It is similar to a person scoring higher marks because they have read a textbook many times."

In addition, reading the a book for the second time is more interesting because the sentiment of that day depends the feeling after reading the book. Even reading the same book, the feeling can be vary when reading it in on a gloomy day or in on a very exciting day. We can see different parts of each book.

To sum up, I think the second time of reading the a book would be more entertaining than the first time because we can look at the book in the a different vision. Finding another face of the a book is the most enjoyable part in reading the a book. In this way, reading in the second time is the 'real' reading.

- This is not entirely clear. Do you mean that after you read a book you feel different, or do you mean that your mood at the time when you read a book influences what you get from the book?

- This needs to be expanded to make it directly relevant to the idea of the paragraph. "We can see different parts of a book depending on our emotion and state of mind when we read it."

- This is a good conclusion, but just make sure that you include exactly the points you mentioned in your body paragraphs.

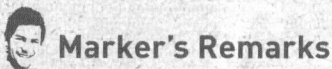 **Marker's Remarks**

Overall, this is a very good piece of writing. Most of your sentences and phrases are constructed correctly and clearly, and you have directly answered the question. You have used good transitions between the paragraphs, and the paragraphs contain solid and well-presented arguments.

In terms of use of English, there are just a few points to work on. First, try to avoid writing in the first person if you can. Second, make sure you know how to use the article correctly. Third, try to avoid beginning sentences with conjunctions (unless you are really trying to emphasize something).

Also, look at your structure. The introduction is very long compared to your body paragraphs. Think about how you could use your experience of 'The Little Prince' as validation in a body paragraph (which would then be more acceptable to write in the first person).

step 3 Here is the same question answered by a native-English speaker:

Although reading a book for the second time means you know what is coming, the statement that it is more interesting to read a book the second time rather than the first time is true. Firstly, it is easy to miss important parts of a book the first time it is read, and secondly it is possible to gain a deeper knowledge of the meaning of the book in the second reading.

It is very easy to overlook aspects of a book the first time it is read. Some books contain lots of facts, and some novels give readers a lot of subtle clues. It is almost impossible to identify and retain all the significant facts and clues the first time a book is read. For instance, an author like Dan Brown, who wrote 'Angles and Demons,' provides lots of details that seemingly mean nothing yet are vital to the conclusion of the story. During the second time of reading these crucial facets are more easily absorbed, making the book far more appealing.

Secondly, some books are difficult to understand and by reading it twice the reader gets far more enjoyment because he or she comprehends the true meaning. For example, 'The Little Prince' is a book that can be read on two levels. It can just be seen as a book about a young boy trying to get home, or it can be interpreted with a deeper gist about the nature of friendship and the way to live. If a reader studies a book for the second time he or she can appreciate more the deeper and hidden sense of the book, thereby gaining far more enjoyment.

To sum up, a second reading is far more fascinating that the first reading. All parts of the book can be understood, and true meaning can be ascertained.

Exercise 6b

Examine the essay written by the <u>native speaker of English</u> and answer the following questions. See the answer key at the back of the book for explanations.

1 What synonyms and/or alternative phrases were used for the following words:

interesting: ....

important: ....

understanding: ....

2 The introduction does not contain a 'hook.' Try to write a suitable 'hook' for this essay.

....

....

....

....

3 Use this checklist to evaluate both body paragraphs of the essay.

	YES	NO
Is there a clear topic sentence in each paragraph?		
Is there a clear concluding sentence in each paragraph?		
Is there one point per paragraph?		
Is each point supported adequately?		
Do the points directly answer the question?		
Is there a clear transition between the paragraphs?		

Essential Skills

Skill A: Agreeing or disagreeing with a statement without using the words 'agree' and 'disagree'

It is easier to write academically if you can avoid the words 'agree' and 'disagree'. An agree/disagree question specifically asks whether you agree or disagree, so you should try to write impersonally (see Unit 9):

- ☹ I agree with the statement that... because   (first person)
- ☹ Many people concur that... because   (Not your view)
- ☺ The statement that... is true because

Exercise 6c

1 Rewrite this introduction using an impersonal voice. You may change as much vocabulary as you wish. There is a sample answer in the key at the back of the book.

> Q: Playing games teaches us about life. Do you agree or disagree?
>
> Fun is very important for children, and I remember how much I enjoyed playing with my friends. Playing is just fun however. I also recall how I learned to share my toys and how to lead others. Therefore I completely agree that playing games teaches us about life.

....

....

....

....

2 Choose expressions from the box below and write a full thesis statement for each of these questions that <u>disagrees with the question statement</u>. You will need to think of your own reasons for disagreeing, and do not use the word 'disagree.' Sample answers are provided in the key at the back of the book.

> - The statement that...
> - It is not true...
> - ... is incorrect because... and...
> - Although... that (question statement), this statement is not accurate as ... and...
> - While... that (question statement), it is not true.

a. Television has destroyed communication among friends and family.

....

....

....

....

b. Businesses should hire employees for their entire lives.

....

....

....

....

Skill B: Writing the opposite meaning/sentiments of the question statement

If you <u>agree</u> with the question statement, using an opposite meaning or sentiment to the question statement can be a good way to write your introduction.

For example, there is nothing wrong with this thesis statement but it is quite basic.

> Q: Parents are the best teachers for their children.
>
> It is true that parents are the best teachers for their children. Firstly...

By using the opposite meaning, you can write a more sophisticated thesis statement:

> Even though schoolteachers are qualified educators, the statement that parents are the best teachers for their children is correct. Firstly...
>
> Although some people may contend that parents do not make good teachers for their children, it is true that parents are better tutors than schoolteachers because...

In both of these thesis statements, an opposite meaning/sentiment is used to add more depth to the viewpoint.

In STEP 2, Unit 5 you looked at using the transitions for acknowledging another viewpoint, and the same transition words and statements can be used.

> **To acknowledge the other viewpoint before stating your viewpoint:**
> | | | | |
> |---|---|---|---|
> | whereas | granted that | even though | though |
> | while | although | | |

Exercise 6d

Write a thesis statement for each of these questions that <u>agrees with the question statement</u>. State the opposite meaning in your thesis statement and use appropriate transitions. Sample answers are in the key at the back of the book.

1 Do you agree or disagree that progress is always good?

....

....

....

....

2 Luxury goods are worth the high cost. Do you agree or disagree?

....

....

....

....

3 Do you agree or disagree with the following statement? Self-confidence is the most important factor for success in school or at work.

....

....

....

....

Further Practice

Write a _complete essay_ for each of these questions. Once you have completed your essays, use this checklist to evaluate your writing.

Introduction	YES	NO
Is there a 'hook' to engage the reader?		
Is there a clear thesis statement that shows the reasons whether you agree or disagree?		
Has the question statement been included in the thesis statement?		
Have the words 'agree' and 'disagree' been omitted?		
Body paragraphs	**YES**	**NO**
Are there clear topic and concluding sentences?		
Is there one paragraph for the first reason, and is there another paragraph for the second reason?		
Is there sufficient expansion and is there sufficient validation for each reason?		
Is the order in which the points are made the same as in the 'thesis statement'?		
Are there clear transitions between the different parts of the essay?		
Conclusion	**YES**	**NO**
Have I included a clear conclusion transition?		
Have I paraphrased my essay statement?		
Have I made a final comment that responds to the 'hook'?		
Have I made sure there is no new information?		

1 "When people succeed, it is because of hard work. Luck has nothing to do with success." Do you agree or disagree with the quotation above? Use specific reasons and examples to explain your position.

Ideas box:

Agree or Disagree	
Reason 1	
Reason 2	

....

....

....

....

....

....

....

....

....

....

2 Do you agree or disagree with the following statement? People should sometimes do things that they do not enjoy doing. Use specific reasons and examples to support your answer.

Ideas box:

Agree or Disagree	
Reason 1	
Reason 2	

Answers
with Explanations STEP2

Unit 1　Writing Cause and Effect Essays

Exercise 1a　▶ see p. 24

Introduction	YES	NO
Does the introduction provide some background information and a hook?	✓	
Does the thesis statement clearly state a cause, an effect and a solution?	✓	

Body paragraph	YES	NO
Is there an appropriate transition to begin the paragraph?	✓	
Are there a clear topic sentence and a concluding sentence?		✓
Is there sufficient explanation or validation of the solution?		✓

⇨ There is a clear topic sentence, but the paragraph lacks a concluding sentence. There is no development or examples in the writing, just a restatement of the topic sentence.

Conclusion	YES	NO
Is there a clear conclusion transition?		✓
Does it clearly paraphrase the causes, effects and solutions?		✓

⇨ The conclusion fails to summarize the causes, effects and solutions in a coherent and connected manner.

Exercise 1b　▶ see p. 31

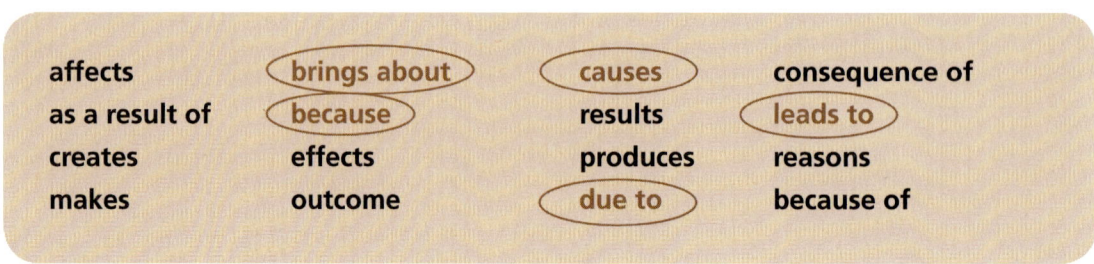

❷ consequently, mean that, contribute to

❸ Type 1 = 'cause and effect' by 'cause and effect'

❹

	YES	NO
Is there a clear topic sentence in each paragraph?	✓	
Is there a clear concluding sentence in each paragraph?	✓	
Is there sufficient 'expansion and explanation' of the topic sentence?	✓	
Is the order in which the points are made the same as in the 'thesis statement'?	✓	
Is each point adequately validated?	✓	
Is there a clear transition between the two paragraphs?		✓

❺ The essay does a good job of explaining two factors that cause obesity in children (lack of exercise and poor diet). However, it does not mention the implications of the obesity rate increasing, which could be things like 'increased cost of medical care' and 'governments needing to spend more money on food education.'

Exercise 1c ▶ see p. 33

❶

a. Parents spend less time at home / <u>children who have little respect for elders</u>

b. <u>unable to sleep properly</u> / drinking too much caffeine

c. <u>inflation</u> / rising oil prices

d. lots of practice / <u>winning the game</u>

e. reading a newspaper every day / <u>increased knowledge of current affairs</u>

f. <u>being punished</u> / being naughty

2

a. Children often have little respect for elders because their parents spend less time at home.

b. Due to drinking too much caffeine I was unable to sleep properly.

c. Rising oil prices cause inflation.

d. Because of lots of practice, Jamie is winning the game.

e. As a result of reading a newspaper every day, a person can increase his or her knowledge of current affairs.

f. Being naughty leads to being punished.

Exercise 1d ▶see p. 36

1
a. Growing up in the countryside is good <u>because of</u> the clean air.
b. <u>Because</u> young people are not interested in traditional crafts, many skills are being lost.
c. <u>Because of</u> the increase in greenhouse gases, the climate is getting warmer.
d. Many people move to cities <u>because</u> there are more job opportunities.
e. Mountain climbing is considered a great hobby <u>because</u> the views from the top are amazing.

2
a. <u>Because</u> they pollute the environment, factories should pay more taxes.
b. <u>Because of</u> the fresh air, people like to live by the sea.
c. <u>Because</u> there is too much data, tables of information are hard to describe.

3
a. The country became very powerful <u>because</u> many people moved there.
b. Many birds have lost their natural habitats <u>because of</u> deforestation.
c. Many poor people will have even more financial hardship <u>because of</u> the change in the tax law.

Unit 2   Writing Advantages/Disadvantages Essays

Exercise 2a ▶ see p. 48

Introduction	YES	NO
Is there an opening sentence that includes a 'hook'?	✓	
Is there an essay statement rather than a thesis statement?	✓	
Is there an equal number of advantages and disadvantages?	✓	
Have opinions and preferences been omitted?		✓

⇨ The words "Therefore, people should make more use of public transport." give the writer's opinion.

Body paragraph	YES	NO
Are there a clear topic sentence and a concluding sentence?		✓
Are there clear transitions between each of the disadvantages?		✓

⇨ The topic sentence does not state that the paragraph is about the disadvantages, and it does not inform the reader there will be two points. There is no expansion or validation of either disadvantage, and there are no transitions.

Conclusion	YES	NO
Is there a clear conclusion transition?	✓	
Does it paraphrase the essay statement?		✓
Have opinions and preferences been omitted?	✓	

⇨ The conclusion does not contain all the points from the essay statement.

Exercise 2b   ▶ see p. 54

❶ advantages: improvements, benefits
community: neighbourhood, district, area
disadvantages: drawbacks, negative aspects, problems
university: higher education establishment, higher education facility, campus
residents: local populace, inhabitants, locals, local people

❷ conversely, one of the primary, furthermore, the third main, on the other hand, another negative, lastly, in conclusion, however

❸ The two main problems with this essay are the use of the first person (for instance 'my community' instead of 'a community'), and there are opinions given in the concluding sentence of each paragraph.

Exercise 2c   ▶ see p. 56

Answers will vary.

❶ Ideas box:

Advantages	Priority	Disadvantages	Priority
Low maintenance	3	High initial cost	1
Low ongoing costs	2	Requires lots of sun	2
Environmentally friendly	1	No energy made at night	3

Essay statement of the introduction:
Solar energy has many advantages and disadvantages. On the positive side it is environmentally friendly, it does not cost much to maintain and it is low maintenance. However, solar energy costs a lot to implement, it needs a great deal of sunshine and it does not make energy at nighttime.

❷ Ideas box:

Advantages	Priority	Disadvantages	Priority
Better school spirit	2	Lack of individuality	3
Reduces conflict	3	Often expensive	1
Promotes discipline	1	Only worn at school	2

Essay statement of the introduction:
Wearing a school uniform is good in that it increases discipline, creates a sense of community, and helps to reduce conflict. On the other hand, school uniforms are often expensive, they can only be worn at school and they diminish a person's individuality.

Exercise 2d ▶ see p. 59

❶ The essay statement contains the opinion that living in a big city is preferable to living in the countryside. Also, the question is about the advantages and disadvantages of living in a big city, it is not asking you to compare a big city to the countryside.

Paraphrase or alternative of the opening sentence	As technology develops and becomes more important in our lives, people tend to move to big cities for work instead of staying in the countryside.
New essay statement with no opinion or preference	It is easy to meet people and life is convenient in a big city, however big cities can be polluted and noisy.

❷ This essay statement implies the author's preference by using the word 'Although' and by giving two disadvantages but only one advantage.

Paraphrase or alternative of the opening sentence	Nuclear power is a potential answer to one of the biggest challenges facing the human race–how to produce more energy while reducing the consumption of fossil fuels.
New essay statement with no opinion or preference	Nuclear power has some drawbacks in that it is hard to store the radioactive waste and it can be dangerous, but is advantageous in that it is cheap and does not emit many harmful greenhouse gases.

Unit 3   Writing Compare and Contrast Essays

Exercise 3a   ▶ see p. 77

❶

Introduction	YES	NO
Does the introduction include a hook?		✓
Does the thesis statement state the topic, the items to be described about the topic, and is it clear whether the essay is a comparison, a contrast, or both?	✓	

❷

Body paragraph	YES	NO
Is there an appropriate transition to begin the paragraph?	✓	
Is there a clear topic sentence and is there a concluding sentence?	✓	
Is there sufficient explanation and is there sufficient validation?	✓	

❸

Conclusion	YES	NO
Is there a clear conclusion transition?	✓	
Does it state the topic and the items of difference?	✓	

Exercise 3b   ▶ see p. 85

❶ easy: straightforward, uncomplicated
difficult: demanding, hard, arduous, challenging
class: lessons, lecture, program
student: learner, undergraduate, person
differences: distinctions, disparities

❷ Type 2 - 'comparison paragraph' and 'contrast paragraph'

❸

	YES	NO
Is there a clear topic sentence in each paragraph?		✓
Is there a clear concluding sentence in each paragraph?		✓
Is there sufficient 'expansion and explanation' of the topic sentence?		✓
Is the order in which the points are made the same as in the 'thesis statement'?		✓
Is each point adequately validated?		✓
Is there a clear transition between the two paragraphs?	✓	

⇨ The first body paragraph does not have a clear topic sentence, and neither body paragraph has a strong concluding sentence. The expansion and validation are insufficient in the first body paragraph.

❹ The conclusion contains an opinion and does not state the similarities and differences.

Exercise 3c ▶ see p. 88

Answers will vary.

❶ Exercising at the gym and jogging in the park share many common traits. They are similar in that a person can increase their heart rate, and in that a person can build up his or her muscles.

❷ Keeping fish is very different from keeping dogs as pets. Firstly, a dog needs far more attention than fish, and fish are much cheaper to look after than dogs.

❸ Watching sport and playing sport are the same in some ways yet different in others. They are similar in that there is a sense of excitement in both watching and playing, but different in that playing sport requires far more dedication.

Exercise 3d ▶ see p.91

❶ Learning in the classroom is very much like studying on the Internet. Teachers prepare the lesson content for both classroom-based instruction and Internet lessons, and Internet-based instruction uses the same multimedia resources as a teacher in the class.

❷ It is not the same to live in university accommodation and to live off-campus. Firstly, living in the campus gives a person more opportunity to meet other people and join in social activities. Secondly, living outside the university is far less convenient as the student needs to travel much further for his or her lectures.

Unit 4 — Writing Opinion Essays

Exercise 4a ▶ see p. 106

❶

Introduction	YES	NO
Is there an opening sentence that includes a 'hook'?		✓
Does the thesis statement clearly state the writer's opinion?	✓	
Does the thesis statement give at least two valid reasons for the opinion?		✓
Is the opinion written in the third person?		✓

⇨ This introduction does not give a valid reason to support the thesis statement, and there is only one reason given. "I think" is the first person.

❷

Body paragraph	YES	NO
Is there a clear topic sentence and is there a concluding sentence?		✓
Does the writer 'expand and explain' the topic sentence?		✓
Is there sufficient support and is there sufficient validation for the opinion?		✓
Is there only one opinion given in the paragraph?		✓

⇨ The topic sentence is a little weak and there is no concluding sentence. The support is not directly related to topic sentence, and the paragraph contains more than one point.

3

Conclusion	YES	NO
Is there a clear conclusion transition?	✓	
Does it restate the writer's opinions?	✓	
Is there a final comment?	✓	

Exercise 4b ▶ see p. 113

1 development: enhance, improve, expand, learn, gain, advance
essential: necessary, compulsory, required
abroad: overseas, another country, other countries, foreign

2 The introduction has a good hook, but it does not contain the reasons why the writer has this opinion. Also, the use of the first person should be avoided if possible.

The conclusion does not have the strongest transition. It does restate the writer's opinion, but it could be expanded to include the reasons. The point about saving money is unrelated to anything else in the essay.

3

	YES	NO
Is there a clear topic sentence in each paragraph?		✓
Is there a clear concluding sentence in each paragraph?	✓	
Are there clear transitions to begin each paragraph?		✓
Does each paragraph contain one opinion that is adequately expanded and explained?	✓	
Is each point adequately validated?	✓	
Is each opinion directly relevant to answering the question?	✓	

⇨ The topic sentence in the first body paragraph is a bit weak; it does not directly link personal development to travel. The first body paragraph does not have a clear transition.

Exercise 4c   ▶ see p. 115

① Making sure people save for their future is a challenge for the government. To ensure that people have adequate retirement arrangements the government should automatically tax a portion of a person's salary and invest this money into a pension on the person's behalf.

② People watch movies for a variety of reasons, including escaping the drudgery of their daily routine. Watching a movie can also help a person learn more about the world.

Exercise 4d   ▶ see p. 118

① For instance, my younger brother plays the piano and now has very dexterous fingers. Not only can he play the piano but also now he is very good at making small and intricate models. He could not have gained this skill from watching TV.

② The fact that music requires a person to learn another 'type of language' illustrates this point. By learning how to read music a child acquires skills that helps him or her to understand mathematical problems and also helps with learning other spoken languages.

③ This point is encapsulated in the famous quotation from Confucius, "Music produces a kind of pleasure which human nature cannot do without."
This saying tells us that a child will get far more benefit from learning to play an instrument than he or she would from watching TV.

Unit 5   Writing Preference Essays

Exercise 5a ▶ see p. 131

Introduction	YES	NO
Does the introduction paraphrase the question?		✓
Is the other statement/opinion acknowledged?		✓
Is there an appropriate transition to introduce the other statement/opinion?		✓
Is there a strong thesis statement?	✓	

⇨ There is no mention in the introduction about spending time playing instead of studying, although the preference of the writer is shown in the thesis statement.

Body paragraph	YES	NO
Is there an appropriate transition to begin the paragraph?	✓	
Is there a clear topic sentence and is there a concluding sentence?		✓
Is there sufficient explanation for the preference?		✓
Is there an example to reinforce the preference?	✓	

⇨ This body paragraph contains an example, but there is no clear topic sentence, no explanation and no concluding sentence.

Conclusion	YES	NO
Is there a clear conclusion transition?	✓	
Does it clearly restate the preference?	✓	
Does it acknowledge the other statement/opinion?	✓	
Does it briefly summarize the reasons for the preference?	✓	

Exercise 5b ▶ see p. 138

1 alone: by themselves, solitude, oneself
motivation: enthusiasm, encouraged
study: cramming, learning
members: peers, participants

2 while, this point can be illustrated by, therefore, furthermore, for example, so, in conclusion, whereas, likewise

3

	YES	NO
Is there a clear topic sentence in each paragraph?	✓	
Is there a clear concluding sentence in each paragraph?	✓	
Is there sufficient 'expansion and explanation' of the topic sentence?	✓	
Is the order in which the points are made the same as in the 'thesis statement'?		✓
Is each point adequately validated?	✓	
Is there a clear transition between the two paragraphs?	✓	

Exercise 5c ▶ see p. 140

Answers will vary.

1

Opposing view	Abroad
Your view	Own country
Reason 1	Prefer food
Reason 2	Can learn more about one's own culture

Your points:
Whereas vacationing abroad can be pleasurable, it is better to have a holiday domestically because people can feel more comfortable eating their home food and they can learn more about their own culture.

Opposing view	Apartment
Your view	House
Reason 1	Less noise
Reason 2	Garden

Your points:
Granted that living in an apartment can be convenient, it is more desirable to live in a house as in a house there is no noise from people living upstairs, and a house usually has a nice garden.

Opposing view	Restaurant
Your view	Home
Reason 1	Know the ingredients
Reason 2	Make exactly as one likes

Your points:
Although it can be fun to visit a restaurant sometimes, it is far better to eat home-cooked food. Firstly, a person knows exactly what ingredients went into the dish when it is prepared at home. Secondly, home-cooked food can be made exactly how a person likes the meal, whereas at a restaurant the dish cannot so easily be altered to a person's particular taste.

Exercise 5d ▶ see p. 143

Answers will vary.

❶ Sometimes, reading a novel is a good way to spend some time. However, reading non-fiction is more advisable as it is possible to learn more useful facts and non-fiction is better composed.

❷ Having friends and knowing where everything is are two reasons why it is better to stay in a hometown than it is to move to another place.

❸ It is advisable to wake up early rather than late.

Unit 6　Writing Agree/Disagree Essays

Exercise 6a　▶ see p. 156

Introduction	YES	NO
Is there an opening sentence that includes a 'hook'?	✓	
Is there a strong thesis statement that includes the question statement and explicit reasons?		✓
Is the introduction written in the third person?		✓

⇨ The hook is a little bit weak. The thesis statement does include the question statement but it does not give reasons. The introduction should not contain examples.

Body paragraph	YES	NO
Is there a clear topic sentence and is there a concluding sentence?	✓	
Is there sufficient expansion of the topic sentence?		✓
Is there sufficient and appropriate validation of the reason?		✓

⇨ The topic and concluding sentences are about asking for money to be returned, but the expansion and validation are about a slightly different topic. As the validation is a personal experience the use of the first person is OK, but contractions should always be avoided.

Conclusion	YES	NO
Is there a clear conclusion transition?	✓	
Does it paraphrase the essay statement, including specific reasons?	✓	
Does it answer the hook?	✓	

⇨ The conclusion includes reasons and the question statement, but it is not paraphrased. It does answer the hook, but it should not be written in the first person if possible.

Exercise 6b ▶ see p. 163

Answers will vary.

❶ interesting: appealing, enjoyment, fascinating
important: significant, crucial
understanding: knowledge, meaning, absorbed, comprehends, interpreted, ascertained

❷ One of the best things about books is that a person can keep a book for his or her entire life, and a book can be enjoyed more than once.

❸

	YES	NO
Is there a clear topic sentence in each paragraph?	✓	
Is there a clear concluding sentence in each paragraph?	✓	
Is there one point per paragraph?	✓	
Is each point supported adequately?	✓	
Do the points directly answer the question?	✓	
Is there a clear transition between the paragraphs?	✓	

Exercise 6c ▶ see p. 164

Answers will vary.

❶ Most people can recall playing and having fun as children. But these experiences provide more than just entertainment; playing games teaches people about life. Through games, people learn about compromise and sharing, and they also learn leadership skills.

❷

a. While it is often said that television has destroyed communication among friends and family, it is not true. Watching a TV programme can lead to debate, and often people are excluded from a discussion if they have not watched a particular program.

b. The statement that a business should hire employees for a person's entire life is not correct, primarily because it is impossible for a business to know if a person will remain productive throughout his or her life. Also, businesses need to change to survive and if it had to guarantee employment to someone the business would find it harder to be competitive.

Exercise 6d ▶ see p. 167

Answers will vary.

❶ Whereas some people like tradition and believe that the world was a better place in the past, it cannot be denied that progress is always beneficial. Without progress people would die younger, have much poorer living conditions and they would not be able to overcome difficulties as easily as they can now do.

❷ Granted that some luxury items are very expensive, the statement that these goods are worth the high cost is correct. Firstly, luxury goods are made using superior materials, and secondly, owning luxury goods provide a person with a sense of achievement and pride.

❸ The statement that self-confidence is the most important factor for success in school or at work is correct. Although some people may argue that luck and hard work and dedication are vital, self-confidence is more important for the following reasons. Firstly, shy people cannot get recognition no matter how clever they are, and confidence can easily make up for any lack of other skills.